UNFORGETTABLE
GARDENS

UNFORGETTABLE
GARDENS

500 YEARS OF HISTORIC GARDENS AND LANDSCAPES

**EDITED BY
SUSANNAH CHARLTON**

BATSFORD

Contents

OPPOSITE Wrest Park, Bedfordshire.
PREVIOUS PAGE Althelhampton, Dorset.

Introduction

OPPOSITE The world's oldest topiary gardens, dating back to the 1690s, at Levens Hall, Cumbria.

The UK has the finest collection of historic parks, gardens and designed landscapes in the world, something of which we can be truly proud. They range from the grandest stately homes, outstanding private gardens, and botanic gardens to public parks and even cemeteries. Some are managed by public bodies, such as the National Trust, English Heritage, and local authorities. Others are cared for by private owners, charitable trusts and volunteers. They embody our rich history of garden-making from the 16th century right up to the present day. They also provide much-valued quiet spaces to escape to for wellbeing, recreation and reflection.

The gardens in this book are just a selection. All are special, equally unforgettable, but vulnerable to change. A primary purpose of the Gardens Trust is to protect and conserve them for present and future generations. As any gardener knows, no garden is ever finished. Always, it is evolving. Without constant care and attention, it will rapidly fall into neglect and become an overgrown wilderness. Then, all too easily, it will be lost for future generations to enjoy. Parks and gardens are also under constant threat from development. This may cause significant harm directly, or more insidiously, by damaging their character, their setting and sense of tranquillity. Ill-considered change can so easily cause irretrievable harm. That is why the protection of historic parks and gardens matters so much.

The Gardens Trust was formed ten years ago when the Garden History Society and the Association of County Gardens Trusts merged. Today, it works in association with the 36 County Gardens Trusts spread across England, the Welsh Historic Gardens Trust and Scotland's Garden and Landscape Heritage. It plays a vital role in protecting our historic parks and gardens. In 1983, Parliament created a Register of Historic Parks and Gardens of Special Significance, recognizing that they are a fragile and finite resource; Scotland and Wales have their own systems of designation and protection. The creation of the Register was in response to a campaign, persistently and valiantly fought, by the Trust's predecessors. We are celebrating the fortieth anniversary of the first entries to the Register in 2024, and today there are over 1,700 sites entered on it. Almost all the parks and gardens featured in this book appear there. In 2023, Parliament accepted that there was a need for further protection and legislated to impose a requirement on all planning authorities, when deciding whether or not to grant planning permission, to have regard to the desirability of preserving or enhancing the registered site or its setting. We have yet to see what difference this will make in practice, but it provides an important additional safeguard in a time of rapid change and pressure to release more land for building.

The role of the Gardens Trust has never been more important. Within the English planning system, it is a statutory consultee. This gives it the right to be consulted on any application that affects a site on the Register and to make representations on whether the proposed development should be permitted or not. We could not fulfil this huge responsibility without the hard work of our volunteers, both within the Trust and the County Gardens Trusts around the country. Together, they provide essential support to our small but dedicated conservation team. However, this protection only extends to sites that are on the Register. We therefore support research which helps to uncover and record the history of other significant parks and gardens and advocate for them to be added to the Register.

It is not just historic gardens that need protection. New gardens of today can be historic gardens of tomorrow. In 2020 we worked with Historic England to identify post-war gardens and landscapes deserving protection. As a result, 20 new sites were added to the Register, including public

parks, the gardens of housing estates and the landscapes of a factory, university college and offices. You will find articles on several of them in this book: Campbell Park in Milton Keynes, Denmans Garden in West Sussex and Beth Chatto Gardens in Essex. More recently, we organized a project that enabled volunteers to research important historic parks and gardens in Suffolk. This has resulted in seven gardens and landscapes being added to the list, including Thorpeness Meare, England's first purpose-built holiday village.

One garden in this book, Painswick Rococo Garden in Gloucestershire, was rediscovered after its owners read an article in the Gardens Trust journal, *Garden History*, by historians Timothy Mowl and Roger White. They had been inspired to write about it having seen a painting of the garden. The bones of this delightful 18th-century pleasure ground, together with its many garden buildings, were revealed beneath a modern conifer plantation. Other landscapes have benefitted from the careful, considered advice of our conservation team, helping to guide necessary change in a way that minimizes the impact on the landscape and its historical significance.

We are keen to encourage more people to enjoy and recognize the value of these gardens and landscapes, by sharing our knowledge, organizing events, online talks and in-person visits, and by recruiting and training volunteers. You can find more information about all we do, or how to join us or support our work on our website: thegardenstrust.org.

The Gardens Trust is immensely grateful to all the historians and experts who have given their time to contribute to this book. The landscapes, parks and gardens described here in the essays and 50-odd individual entries are just a small and necessarily partial selection. There are many, many other inspiring places that could have been included. Now it is time to dip in and enjoy! We hope the book will inspire you to visit some of these unforgettable gardens, and that you will want to join us in supporting them. The protection and conservation of our heritage of historic parks and gardens has never been more important, and we need all the support we can get for the work that we do.

Peter Hughes, Chairman, the Gardens Trust

GARDENS IN THE 16ᵀᴴ CENTURY

The quest for gardens before about 1500 is tantalizing because there are no survivals. While a small number of sites have been revealed by archaeology, and there are a few modern reconstructions, most gardening would have been for food crops and basic medicine. Examples of such gardening can be seen at the Weald & Downland Living Museum in West Sussex.

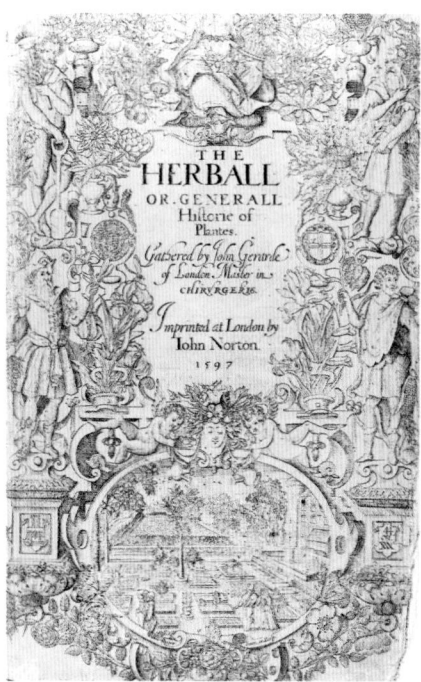

The late 15th century was a turning point globally with European exploration opening up trade routes to Asia and the Americas. In England, the Battle of Bosworth in 1485 marked the end of the Wars of the Roses, and the accession of Henry Tudor bought relative civil peace for the first time in a hundred years. This meant fewer military expenses, and more taxes paid, so the amount of time and money that the Crown and small band of the nobility and other elite had at their disposal increased immensely. Castles became redundant and new fine domestic residences no longer needed to be fortified, so new architectural fashions could be employed.

Although Henry VII himself had a well-deserved reputation for being fiscally prudent, when he rebuilt the royal palace at Richmond, he spared no expense. Described as 'the bright and shining star of building' he surrounded it with elaborate gardens. While many of the features – such as the 'carpentry work', mazes, raised beds and mounts – grew out of well-established medieval traditions, there were innovations too. Galleries, two-storied and made of wood, ran around the perimeter, offering space for entertainment as well as easy access to the gardens, which were planted with 'many vines, seeds and strange fruits'. They also contained heraldic animals 'carved into the ground right well sanded and compassed in with lead' as well as 'Rampande Lyons, stode up wonderfly, / Made all of herbes, with dulcet swetenes'.

Richmond was the first of a series of great early Tudor palaces which included Hampton Court, Nonsuch,

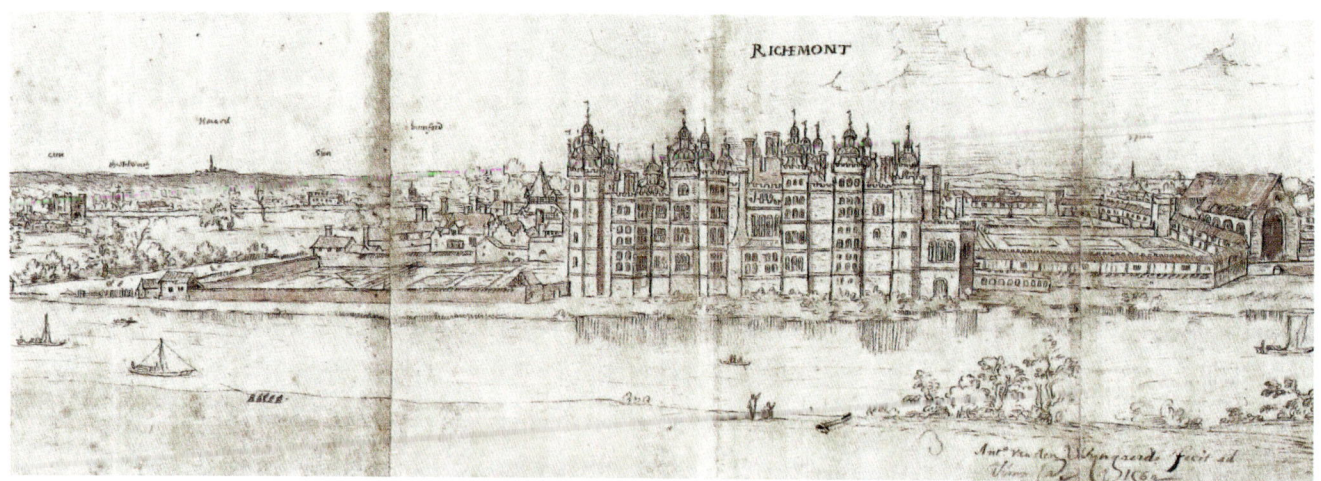

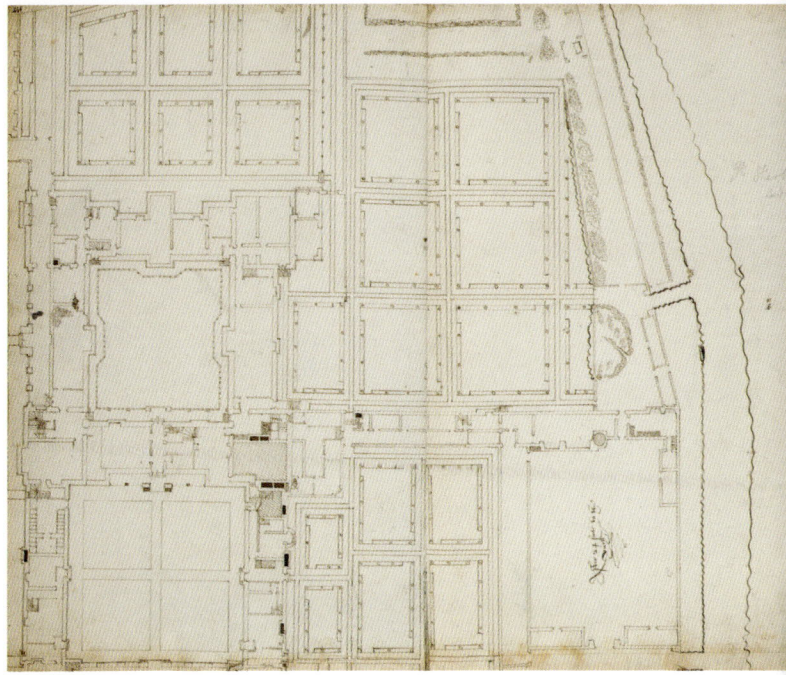

Greenwich and Oatlands. In those the heraldic theme was developed by Henry VIII with widespread use of brightly coloured Royal Beasts, usually seated on pillars, taking pride of place. Each was a visual reminder of the Tudors' connection to earlier dynasties and were a way of reinforcing their place in history and their own dynastic ambitions.

Henry VII and his son Henry VIII reformed the government and in doing so created a class of professional administrators to run it, who were dependent on the Tudors for their positions and wealth. Royal building and garden-making cost money and when the treasury was empty Henry VIII, supported by these 'new men' organized the seizure of the wealth of England's monasteries. This provided a massive injection of property ripe for conversion or demolition for building materials, as well as of money. It led to a massive wave of new building and garden-making.

Some monastic buildings, such as Laycock Abbey, were remodelled for residential use, others were demolished and the materials recycled in grand new houses, such as Hengrave Hall. Meanwhile, castles such as Framlingham, Raglan and St Donat's, were being domesticated with formal gardens laid out outside their once defensive walls.

Although the political and religious uncertainty of the mid-century led to a pause in building, it resumed again early in the reign of Elizabeth I. This time it was not the Crown who led the way but the queen's courtiers. Headed by her chief minister William Cecil, Lord Burghley, and her Lord Chancellor, Christopher Hatton, aristocratic palaces sprang up all round the country, including a veritable roll-call of our favourite stately homes: Burghley, Holdenby,

Kirby, Longleat, Wollaton, Montacute and Hardwick. They were the match of anything in Europe. Very quickly they were copied on a smaller scale by both country gentry and the City of London's commercial elite.

William Cecil built not just one but three grand houses. He had a large town house on the Strand in central London, plans of which are the oldest extant garden designs, while Burghley near Stamford was his country base. Even more spectacular though must have been his long-destroyed palace at Theobalds in Hertfordshire, which was, according to visitors, 'of immense extent ... where a man might walk two miles before he came to their ends.' They contained imported Italian sculpture, labyrinths, summerhouses, 'columns and pyramids of wood and other material' a fountain where 'the water spouts out from a number of concealed pipes and sprays unwary passers-by,' and even 'a ship floating on the water complete with cannons, flags and sails'.

Matching Theobalds in extent, if not contents, was Holdenby in Northamptonshire, the largest house in the

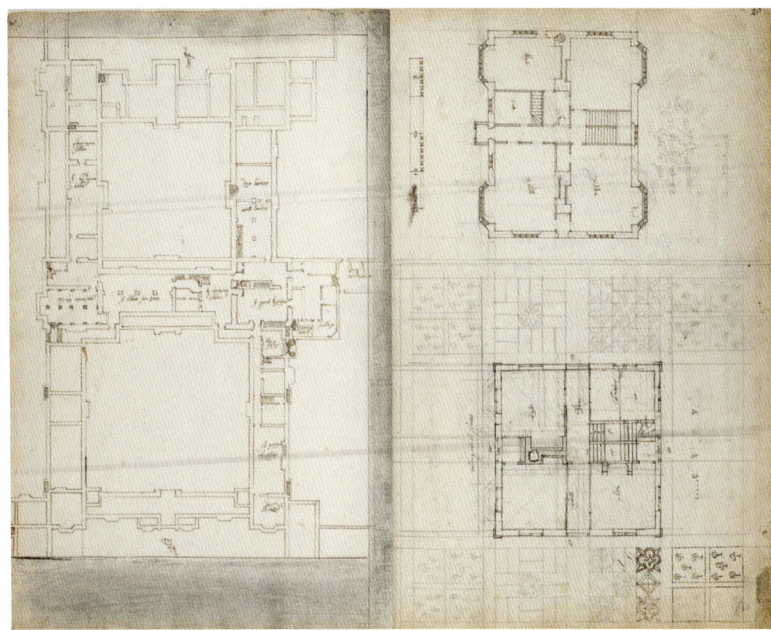

country and quite possibly in Western Europe, built for Hatton. Its garden was beautifully surveyed by Ralph Treswell twice in the 1580s, and although the palace was largely demolished in the mid-17th century, the remains of the garden can still be made out in parts and are there waiting for the archaeologists to uncover.

The architecture of these prodigy houses, as they became known, staggered the viewer with their scale, their great expanses of glass, and their openness to their surroundings. As John Thorpe's plan for Dowsby in Lincolnshire shows, the garden was now beginning to be designed integrally with the mansion. It was no longer an afterthought, but the setting for the architectural jewel that was the new house, which sat in a network of connected and carefully planned spaces that were designed to impress and overawe visitors. Usually approached through vast deer and hunting parks, the house was reached through a series of increasingly formal courts, perhaps with grand entrance arches, such as at Holdenby, as the house came into view.

Prodigy house gardens were often not visible on the approach but only once inside. They were designed to be as spectacular as the architecture, often taking the simple geometric designs shown in early gardening and architectural books and playing with them, mathematically or philosophically, as Thomas Tresham did at Lyveden in Northamptonshire. Contemporary images often show repeated geometric beds – usually square, but frequently with varied patterns of internal planting. They show, too, long arboured tunnels and walks, banqueting houses, prospect mounts, statues, topiary, canals and fountains. Heraldic Beasts are no longer quite so evident but were installed on a smaller scale at Kenilworth, Warwickshire, in 1575 and they have since always been seen as 'typically Tudor' in later recreations such as St Donat's in the Vale of Glamorgan.

By the later 16th century, England had become less isolated, as the elite travelled more, collected, and read books in foreign languages, while Continental books were also translated faster. Particularly important were architectural books, such as those of Sebastiano Serlio or Vitruvius, with collections of designs that could be used interchangeably for embroidery, wall panelling, plasterwork and garden design. Garden makers such as Thomas

Tresham of Lyveden, William Cecil and Christopher Hatton had large libraries including many of these architectural texts but are also known to have collected plans and architectural drawings to draw upon for their projects.

At the same time the range of plants available was increasing too. Elizabeth I, and later James I, encouraged merchants and adventurers to explore the world, particularly North America, and started the first colonies. Inevitably this led to new plant introductions from the potato and tobacco to the pumpkin and the chilli, the crown imperial (*Fritillaria imperialis*) and the tulip to the sunflower, and the so-called French and African marigolds. These new plants are recorded in John Gerard's *Herball* of 1597, which shows that such new exotic plants were becoming collectable items. While it's difficult to be precise about the dates of introduction, the Stradling family probably grew the first tomatoes and other solanums in Britain at St Donat's before 1590.

The turn of the 16th and 17th centuries was the beginning of the age of collectors and consumers – novelty and wealth provided the opportunity to show off your knowledge and learning, new discoveries and a fascination with nature. The aristocratic elite of late Elizabethan and Jacobean England were early victims of consumerism, and gardens were one of the ways they consumed. It meant that gardens became places to show off their wealth, status and education. We know from contemporary publications by her courtiers that the gardens served – at Kenilworth, Theobalds and Elvetham, Hampshire, among many others – as backdrops for extravagant entertainment for the queen on her progresses. They were often proudly included in the backgrounds to portraits in stark contrast to the standard dark background of earlier Tudor portrayals. In her own portraits, which were all carefully stage-managed and controlled, Elizabeth used plants and flowers as symbols. Her adoption of the eglantine rose as her personal flower helped develop the cult of Gloriana, as exemplified by Nicholas Hilliard's miniature, 'Young Man Among Roses'.

Yet all this is achieved with very little advance from preceding centuries in horticultural technology, knowledge or skill. These do not change until the arrival of large numbers of Huguenot refugees, fleeing religious persecution in France and the Low Countries from the 1550s onwards. Over the following century, they helped transform England's commercial gardening, introducing new techniques, ideas and crops, boosting food production, and eventually helping gardening become a recognized profession, with the establishment of the Worshipful Company of Gardeners in 1605.

The Tudor garden was marked by complex designs, extravagantly made features, beautiful objects and brilliant colours that helped make up for the lack of plant variety, all of which meant that the 16th century truly was a golden age of garden-making.

David Marsh

The Elizabethan Garden Kenilworth Castle

Robert Dudley, Earl of Leicester (1532–88), created the most significant of Kenilworth's gardens, recorded in a detailed letter by Robert Langham describing a stay by Queen Elizabeth I in July 1575. In 1563 she had granted Dudley, her favourite, the titles Earl of Leicester and Baron Denbigh, as well as Kenilworth Castle and other property. Leicester refurbished the castle, building a new wing, gate-house and garden influenced by the latest European thinking.

While the Queen was out hunting, Adrian the gardener let Langham view the garden. His letter described the garden as having a raised terrace, 'ten foot high and twelve broad', with fine arbours 'redolent by sweet trees and flowers' at each end. The balustrade was decorated with obelisks, spheres and white bears, and sand paths were 'smooth and firm, pleasant to walk on as on a seashore when the water is availed [has retreated]'. The garden was in four equal quarters, each with a porphyry obelisk topped by an orb at the centre. The planting was 'deliciously variable' with scented flowers, fragrant herbs and 'fruit-trees bedecked with their apples, pears and ripe cherries'. Apart from the fruit, the garden is not designed for culinary or medicinal use, but purely to please the senses.

Against the north wall a large aviary for songbirds had a cornice 'beautified with great diamonds, emeralds, rubies and sapphires, pointed, tabled, rock and round': set in 'gold by skilful head and hand'. Inside, two holly trees provided shade and perches. At the centre 'a very fair fountain cast into an eight square, reared a four foot high' of 'rich hard marble', surmounted by two 'atlantes' holding

Warwickshire
–
Robert Langham
–
c. 1570–75
–
Registered Grade II*

RIGHT Reconstruction painting showing an aerial view of Kenilworth Castle as seen from the north, as it may have appeared at the time of Queen Elizabeth I's visit to Kenilworth in 1575.

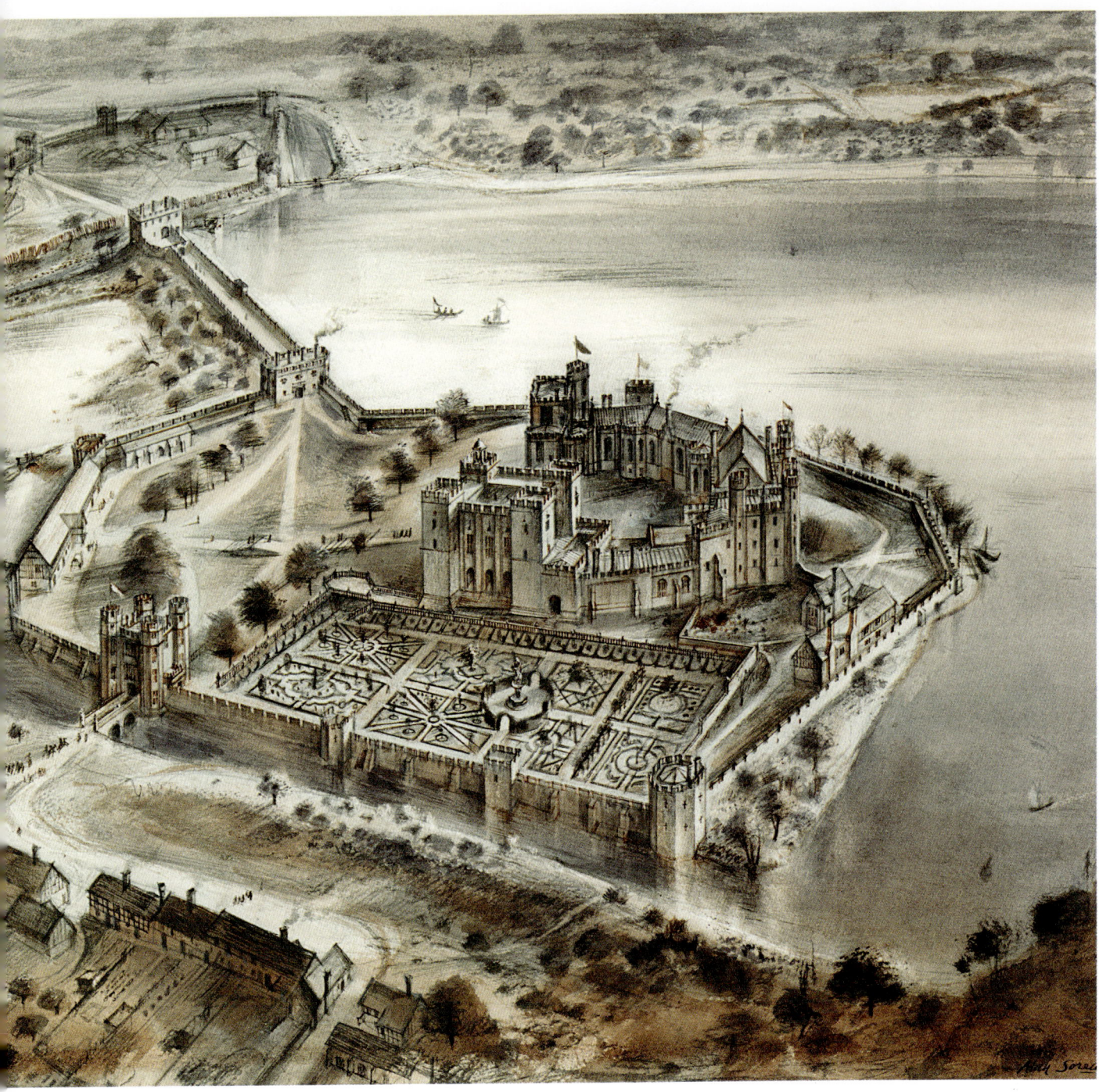

a large ball 'from whence sundry fine pipes stream water to the pool below'. The letter also describes five of the eight panels that form the pool, carved with stories from Ovid's *Metamorphoses*; the Earl of Leicester was patron of the first English translation.

After Leicester's death, the son of James I, Henry, Prince of Wales, bought the castle, which was then inherited by his brother Prince Charles. It became a Parliamentary garrison and was made defensively 'untenable' in 1650. After the Restoration it was left a ruin and the gatehouse became a farmhouse. From the early 18th century Kenilworth

became valued as a romantic ruin and Sir Walter Scott's novel *Kenilworth* (1821) made it a tourist attraction. John Davenport Siddeley, by 1939 1st Baron Kenilworth, transferred the castle to the Office of Works. Archaeology in the 1970s found no evidence of a garden, and William Dugdale's 1656 plan of the castle was used as a basis for a new garden, planted with box-edged beds and yew topiary.

By 1990 this was in poor condition and from 2006 English Heritage investigated reconstructing the Elizabethan garden with a team of experts, including archaeologists, historians and plantsmen. Geophysical

archaeological investigations and a full excavation uncovered the fountain's structure, with chips of white Carrara marble still attached, and the position of the northern curtain wall. The major findings all corroborated Langham's letter.

It was decided to build a new garden based on the archaeology and Langham's letter. Completed in 2009, we are now learning how to manage an Elizabethan garden fit for a queen.

John Watkins

ABOVE The view looking over the Elizabethan Garden to Leicester's Gatehouse at Kenilworth Castle.

OPPOSITE Fountain at the centre of the garden at Kenilworth.

St Donat's Castle

Glamorgan

-

Sir Edward Stradling

-

Late 16th century

-

Registered Grade I

OPPOSITE The Edwardian Rose Garden on a lower terrace of the Tudor garden.

BELOW A postcard of the Rose Garden from 1926.

The garden of St Donat's Castle is one of the grandest, best preserved and most important 16th-century gardens in Britain. The position is spectacular, 'descending', as Samuel and Nathaniel Buck described in 1740, 'in Terrasses from ye Castle Wall to ye Severn Sea; which forms a most glorious Canal between it and Somersetshire.'

The castle was largely built in the 14th and 15th centuries by the Stradling family, while the garden was created in the second half of the 16th century by Sir Edward Stradling (1529–1609), a wealthy Renaissance man who moved in court and scholarly circles.

The main garden is formally laid out in five massive terraces, with flights of steps between them, which drop 40 metres (130 feet) from the castle to the sea wall, also built by Sir Edward. The retaining and revetment walls are massive, built of the local Lias limestone. At the bottom is a level area and another terrace, labelled 'Garden' on the earliest, 1818, plan of the garden. To the west the ground drops steeply to a further section of the Tudor garden, a levelled valley floor flanked by two long terraces with a wall between them. This area is labelled 'Orchard' on all the early maps.

Two contemporary poems show that the garden was greatly admired in its day and that it had Italianate features and exotic plants. The first, dating to before Sir Edward's death in 1609, is by Sir John Stradling, Sir Edward's successor. In this Virgilian Latin poem he mentions violets, white lilies, vines and 'glowing' [marble?] columns. The second is by Dr Thomas Leyshon. Originally in Latin, it

RIGHT Edwardian King's Beasts and former well-head seat in the Tudor Garden at St Donat's Castle.

was translated into Welsh by a friend of Sir Edward; the Latin original was lost and it is from a fragment of the Welsh version that it is known. Leyshon mentions bees, 'gleaming' stones above gateways, vines, roses and lilies. He singles out for special mention two exotics, 'nards' and 'amomum'. Nards are spike lavender (*Lavandula latifolia*), a south European native, and amomum is winter cherry tree (*Solanum pseudocapsicum*), from America. Leyshon also mentions 'golden apples', the name given at the time to tomatoes. As this poem dates to before 1590, this means that the earliest recorded cultivation of tomatoes in Britain was at St Donat's Castle.

After 1609 the only changes to the garden were minor additions. Its Tudor structure survives in its entirety. Between 1901 and 1909 Morgan Stuart Williams transformed the third terrace into a 'Tudor' garden, with king's beasts on pillars and a seat in the centre, using the well head from the inner court of the castle. A summerhouse was built above the fourth terrace, which became a formal rose garden.

In 1925 the American newspaper tycoon, William Randolph Hearst bought St Donat's and lavished money on the castle. From 1931–36 it was the summer retreat of Hearst and his Hollywood friends. In the garden the only additions were a new pavilion on the fourth terrace and a loggia on the fifth. The castle was put up for sale in 1937 and in 1962 became a school, Atlantic College.

Elisabeth Whittle

Holdenby

The gardens at Holdenby complemented Sir Christopher Hatton's mansion, the largest private dwelling in Elizabethan England. Created for a visit from the queen, Elizabeth never came. In 1580 Hatton commissioned Ralph Treswell to make a survey of his house, gardens and land, now in the Northamptonshire Record Office, along with Treswell's second survey of 1587 to celebrate his new hunting park. Estate maps were often produced to show the boundaries of new parks, which were status symbols, the right to empark being granted by the queen herself. Treswell enlivened the survey with jolly hunters with falcons, deer and cavorting rabbits. These represent the economic benefits of the park: the provision of food, material for clothing, and building materials and fuel from the new plantations. The two surveys are a unique record of the development of an Elizabethan garden.

In 1580 the house was complete, but not the grounds. The village lay to the north-east. To the south were the orchard, a grove, some ponds and, adjacent to the house, 'ye garden' is shown quartered with a central feature, flanked by two areas of narrow, parallel lines, inscribed on each side, 'ye Rosiary'. To the west another garden had nine square compartments, a mount in the north-west corner, and a 'sestern [cistern] house', supplied by a conduit, in the centre of the external wall.

By 1587 the village had been moved, the entrance courts enclosed and completed with a banqueting house and new gateways. In the gardens, the ponds shown in the first survey had been dammed and the water diverted to form a

Holdenby,
Northamptonshire
–
Designer unknown
–
c. 1580–87
–
Registered Grade I

OPPOSITE The Pond Garden.

BELOW The Basecourt Arches from the original palace of Holdenby still stand today.

geometric arrangement of ponds. 'Ye garden' to the south was now more intricately planted and the west garden turned into an orchard. The mount and 'sestern house' remained; a banqueting house seems to have been built on the southern end of the terrace.

Because maps at this time did not include contour lines, we only know from descriptions that the 'rosiaries' were, in fact, narrow terraces leading down the steep hill from the house. The effect was described by John Norden in his *A Delineation of Northamptonshire* (1595):

And above the rest is especially to be noated with what industrye and toyle of man, the garden have been raised, levelled, and formed out of a most craggye and unfitable lande now framed a most pleasante, sweete, and princely place, with divers walks, many ascendings and descendings, replenished

also with manie delightful Trees of Fruite, artificially composed Arbours, and a Destilling House on the west end of the same garden, over which is a Ponde of Water, broughte by conduite pypes, out of the feylde adjoyninge on the west, quarter of a myle from the same howse.

Hatton was a bachelor who also owned nearby Kirby Hall. His successors preferred the latter and, within a century, Holdenby House was in ruins. Nathaniel and Samuel Buck's engraved view of c. 1770 shows the remains of the house and the two magnificent arches that flanked the outer court, based on the designs of Sebastiano Serlio. These two arches, along with extensive earthworks, remain today, dramatically visible in aerial photographs.

Paula Henderson

Lyveden New Bield

Northamptonshire

–

Sir Thomas Tresham

–

c. 1594–1605

–

Registered Grade I

Gardens by their very nature are ephemeral – they inevitably evolve and change, and we rarely see an historic garden in the way that was originally intended. This is what makes Lyveden New Bield so special. This garden was designed and created in the late 16th century by Sir Thomas Tresham, although the project was abandoned on the owner's death in 1605. It has remained virtually undisturbed ever since, allowing today's visitors to experience the garden in much the same way as Sir Thomas' contemporaries would have done.

Walking through the gardens is a journey of discovery. Beginning at the Manor House, the visitor, then and now, walks up through a series of gardens which gradually reveal themselves and the panoramic views over the estate, until they reach the main focus of the garden, the remarkable lodge, or New Bield, at the top.

After leaving the house, the ascending path through the grounds, which in Tresham's time was lined with sycamores and elms, brings the visitor up to the lower orchard. This has been replanted according to the original plans with approximately 300 fruit trees in regular rows and divided into four quarters – an Elizabethan connoisseur's display of fruit cultivation on a grand scale. The lower orchard is bordered to the south by a high terrace, with a mount at either end. From here it is possible to see the full extent of the garden, looking back down over the lower orchard to the house or turning to view the moated orchard above. This, if all had gone according to plan, would have been an unforgettable sight. A series of ten concentric borders,

LEFT The Water Garden.

OPPOSITE The garden lodge at Lyveden New Bield.

planted with cherry and plum trees around the outside and a combination of roses and raspberries in the inner circles. This area was to have been surrounded by four canals, although only three sides of this moat were ever dug out. At the southern corners are two spiral mounts, also surrounded by canals. It is still possible to see the extent of all this today, as apart from the planting in the centre, all the other features remain.

Walking round to the far side of the moated orchard offers the first glimpse of the garden lodge, but stopping to climb one of the spiral mounts, much higher than the prospect mounts on the northern corners of the moated orchard, and accessed by a small wooden footbridge, offers views in all directions as the path winds around to the top. From here, the impressive lodge is clearly revealed, the pinnacle of the garden.

Much has been written about the religious symbolism imbued into the design of this lodge, and most likely into the design of the garden as well. Indeed, much is still to be discovered as archaeological work on the site continues, but what we can be sure of is that Lyveden provides us with the rare spectacle of a wonderful extant Elizabethan garden which, it would be nice to think, Sir Thomas himself might recognize.

Jill Francis

GARDENS IN THE 17ᵀᴴ CENTURY

The moment in 1603 when James VI of Scotland also became James I of England coincided with several innovations in garden and planting design. The other end of the century just preceded the demise of William of Orange, whose elaborate Baroque designs marked a high point in sophistication, and the desire to rank alongside Louis XIV's Versailles. The century in between saw the flourishing of walled formal gardens. It had three characteristic design traditions, sometimes overlapping: the Jacobean, one marked by protestant sobriety, and a third driven by political one-upmanship.

Garden writers of the 17th century provided advice to owners on the best situations and dispositions for prospect, aspect and shelter from wind. The gardener would then transform walled areas into gardens. During the last two decades architects sometimes suggested layouts, and professional garden designers applied themselves to the more spectacular places depicted in the plates by Leonard Knyff and Johannes Kip in their *Britannia Illustrata* (1707).

The Elizabethan tradition – knots, orchards, walls pierced by panelled wooden doors and summerhouses at the corners – was continued at minor country houses. The gatehouse was being replaced by gates and porters' lodges, but once through them a paved 'broad walk' would run between grass plats (lawns) to the door; this arrangement remained standard until the end of the century. At the rear of the garden, pretty summerhouses or corner turrets were part of the architecture of Jacobean gardens, and as late as the 1680s.

Manuals by Gervase Markham and William Lawson in the 1610s and '20s grew from the Elizabethan garden tradition, including the continuing fascination with knots displaying the owner's inventiveness. Gillyflowers, cut evergreens and tender plants would be moved around in pots, while the planting of beds transitioned from annuals and herbaceous flowers to bulbs like tulip and narcissus, requiring an entirely different annual cycle. Herbarists like John Tradescant and John Parkinson imported outlandish bulbs and other plants: even sycamore was welcomed at first.

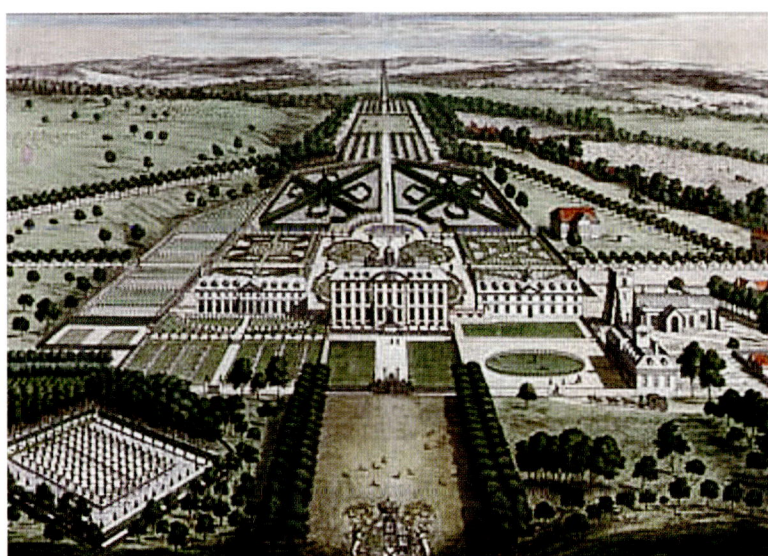

New features in the Jacobean garden included bowling greens, seen from around 1610, and water gardens by Sir Francis Bacon at Gorhambury, Hertfordshire, Sir Walter Cope in Kensington, London, and several others elsewhere. Terracing became fashionable to such an extent that sloping sites were often preferred to level ones for the views they afforded over lower parts of the garden, water bodies and the park beyond. Doors were being replaced by gateways that helped open up the views. 'Mounts' were no longer the conical Tudor ones, but raised walks, sometimes with a grotto underneath, on an axis in the Italian way.

Those affected by the cult of melancholy sought solitude in some wilder place outside the walls. In his essay 'Of Gardens' of 1625 Bacon's ideal garden would have had a 'heath' or 'desert'. Some of these early wildernesses were coppice or other woodland provided with simple seats.

Leading the way with these innovations were members of the royal family and the court, but not James I himself. He was interested in animals, either for their curiosity or for the hunt. He built up a notable collection of rare animals, including camels and crocodiles, and birds in St James's Park and Theobalds in Hertfordshire, and there and elsewhere he greatly expanded his hunting grounds.

Queen Anna employed Salomon de Caus from 1610 to create a Parnassus mountain, in the Florentine style, at Somerset House and an aviary and a reclining goddess at Greenwich Palace. Meanwhile de Caus was serving Prince Henry in preparation for a spectacular water garden at Richmond Palace and was afterwards employed by Princess Elizabeth and the Elector Palatine at Heidelberg. Inigo Jones became the Surveyor of Works in 1615, and his contribution to the royal gardens was elaborate Serlian gateways.

Charles I had a strong interest in sundials and also statuary. He assembled his bronze casts in the garden of St James's. Meanwhile, Queen Henrietta Maria had the services of André Mollet, from the family of French royal gardeners, in making boxwork parterres. She installed a Mollet-style tunnel arbour 80 metres (263 feet) long at Oatlands in Surrey in 1631, and he carried out alterations at Wimbledon Manor in 1640.

The earliest greenhouse for orange trees in England was at Beddington Place to the south of London, with the trees in the ground and the house being re-erected for every winter. Prince Henry had one at St James's and Henrietta-Maria had a permanent brick structure at Wimbledon to which the trees were brought in pots or cases.

OPPOSITE LEFT
Ninepin bowling, a game
related to the more
usual English tradition
of bowls. From William
Lawson, *A New Orchard
and Garden*, 1618.

OPPOSITE
RIGHT Wimpole,
Cambridgeshire, by
Leonard Knyff and
Johannes Kip, 1707, with
its avenue, forecourt,
gardens and open groves.

Axial arrangements were sought, starting with the avenue, then the broad walk, and through the house and garden. Impressive lime avenues planted for the Duke of Buckingham were seen at New Hall, near Chelmsford in Essex, and at Burley-on-the-Hill, Rutland, in the early 1620s. This fashion took hold so that if owners could not arrange a perpendicular frontal approach they planted the avenue trees anyway.

Wilton House, near Salisbury, was the last garden in the Jacobean spirit, made by the Earl of Pembroke in the 1630s, largely for Charles's sake. It had parterres resembling those by the Mollets in France, a grove and a terrace that terminated the scheme with a very elaborate grotto by Salomon de Caus's brother Isaac set into it.

The English Civil War (1642–51) followed by the establishment of the Commonwealth meant there were few new garden projects from 1640 to 1660, because of sequestrations, fines and lack of confidence. Even so, signs of a new approach to gardens were evident.

Gone were terraces, fountains, balustrades, flowerpots, treed walks, arbours and new summerhouses. 'Plain' parterres of grass were preferred in private gardens from the late 1630s, answering the fashion for hard walking and following the examples of London public walks from the late 1600s at Moorfields and Gray's Inn. English skills in keeping bowling greens were put to use and often remarked upon by foreign tourists. Usually the only embellishment was cypress trees at the intersections of the gravel paths.

Flower gardens were henceforward often to the sides of houses. The conservative-minded John Worlidge observed the loss of flowers in the principal garden disapprovingly. However, the architect Hugh May was to remark in the 1660s to Samuel Pepys that the new grass and gravel garden had become the English way.

There were also bowling greens, orchards and other types of garden area to incorporate in layouts. Careful planning could achieve utility plus a rational use of proportions. A garden and its side gardens might be in the proportions of 1:2:1 or another symmetrical arrangement. Examples could be seen at many Commonwealth and Restoration layouts. There were improving books on fruit trees, the best varieties of which were obtained from France and the Netherlands. By the mid-century the training of wall fruit had become an art form, and the number of field orchards and ornamental fruit gardens increased enormously from the 1660s.

The royal residences were sold after the execution of Charles I in 1649, with the intention that they would be demolished, though some (Whitehall, Somerset House, Hampton Court) were kept for government, military and ambassadorial purposes. General Lambert took Wimbledon, assembling a collection of florist varieties; he was parodied as the 'knight of the golden tulip'. Cromwell took Hampton Court and embellished the now-grassed Privy Garden with the fountain basin and statue of Arethusa from Somerset House. Evidently, he was not too concerned about the commandment against graven images.

With the collapse of the radical Protestant regime in 1660, and Charles II's Restoration, austerity could be relaxed as owners sought more interest. Most owners of large gardens continued with square-walled enclosures, but gradually some of the features of the pre-Civil War garden were reintroduced, and new ideas from abroad were experimented with.

Some owners questioned whether gardens always needed to be square, and several were made oblong in shape. An influential example was Cassiobury in Hertfordshire, where Moses Cook was gardener. He described the garden's novel features of a 'great terrace', running across the face of the house, side terraces, and the grate or *grille* at the bottom of the garden, which permitted views of the valley beyond.

In the garden itself, some figures (statues) were imported, usually to serve as centrepieces of grass plats (lawns). Some grottoes and the occasional terrace-mount were made, and flowerpots re-introduced. Many greenhouses were seen. Although André Mollet's designs for parterres were seldom taken up, his advice on axial arrangements influenced a proliferation of avenues, baskethandles and axial vistas beyond the garden.

Deer parks were suggestive of an ancient lineage and thus much prized. Several new ones were created, all in view from the house. A book by Cook of 1676 concerned park embellishment by ridings, avenue systems and their framing of lawns. He also treated the appropriate dimensions of circles and widths of vistas, peripheral planting and *pattes d'oies*. Meanwhile the deer were only occasionally hunted as hunters turned their attention to foxes and the shooting of birds.

The desire to take in views of parkland led to increasing use of forecourt palisades and 'transparent' gates (with iron bars instead of solid panels) from the 1670s, so the far wall opened up and porter's lodges disappeared.

New forms of grove were springing up: not the solitary recess of Jacobean times, but a tidied-up and regularized *bosquet* or groves with high, sheer-sided hedges, contrasting with the flat of the parterre, and to which the term 'wilderness' was transferred. A rarer, variety was the 'open grove', of walks flanked by trees set within shoulder-high hedges allowing views of displays of bulbs or flowering shrubs. Finally, there were evergreen groves which, though encouraged by Mollet and John Evelyn, remained sporadic. Sometimes conifers were the infill of groves, but usually it was trees good for attracting birds, or young forest trees.

Kitchen gardens were becoming a *desideratum* for those following fashions in *cuisine*. Mid-century they had usually been added outside existing walls, but increasingly they became integrated into large new layouts. Often their quarters were hedged with soft fruit, for example gooseberry, but fruit trees were found separately, in fruit gardens.

The pre-Civil War tradition continued, with such innovations, until about 1680 in most English country houses.

Towards the end of the century the leading power in Europe and its leading garden were France and Versailles. Charles II wished to reinstate the reputation of the British crown and embarked on ambitious projects in the royal parks of St James's, Hampton Court and Greenwich Palace.

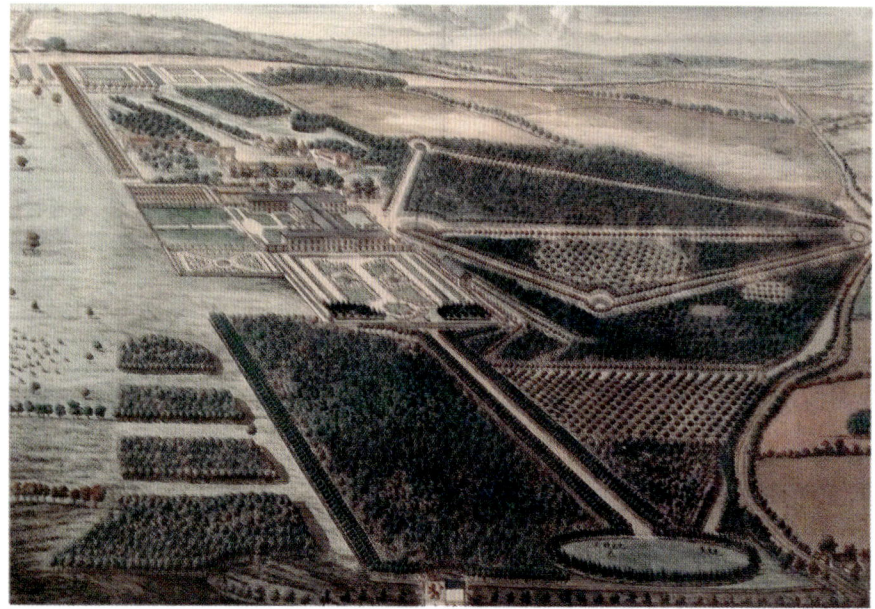

They were to be supervised by influential architect Hugh May's brother, Adrian.

A canal at St James's was flanked by avenues and terminated in a half-moon. The one at Hampton Court was briefly the longest canal anywhere. In addition, a Great Avenue was planted there through Bushy Park, intended to provide a new landward approach to the palace.

André Le Nôtre, who designed the gardens at Versailles, was asked to devise a scheme at Greenwich. He did sketch one out: it would have consisted of an intricate *parterre de broderie*, surrounded by terracing on three sides, and was to be the focus of a network of avenues in the park. This scheme had to be abandoned before the parterre and a grandiose staircase cascade could be made.

A quite separate project was a Royal Garden to be taken out of St James's Park and created by the now elderly Mollet. It was a huge fruit garden of 'dwarf' trees, doubling as a flower garden.

At that time there were few members of the aristocracy that followed Charles's ambitions; the Earl of Arlington was exceptional in his expenditure, creating a hugely impressive forecourt gate and palisade at Euston in Suffolk, a very extensive parterre to the south, terraces and a greenhouse garden to the west. By the end of the 1670s others revived their ambitions and the changes to the Restoration garden were incorporated into a new phase of garden-making much influenced by Versailles.

Flower borders with shaped evergreens around grass plats made what the French called the *parterre a l'Angloise*. Meanwhile, greenhouses were built for exotic plants using the advanced technologies developed in the Netherlands.

A consortium of master gardeners formed a partnership based at Brompton Park, in Kensington, in 1681 in order to supply plants and sometimes make gardens. This nursery had a leading hand in most of the great gardens. Kitchen gardens appears to have been a specialty. Moses Cook was a partner and so was George London, the latter becoming the Royal Gardener in 1689.

Foreign artisans were not infrequently imported to create statuary and ironwork. In several parterres there were fountains of Neptune, tritons or seahorses, and elsewhere great numbers of *jets d'eau*. Reflecting basins might enliven avenues, the forecourt could be invaded by carriage sweeps, and wooden gates replaced by foliate ironwork, or by iron *grilles* that allowed views out. Wildernesses were elaborated with cabinets and curving walks, terraces multiplied, and artificial slopes could tidy up whole hillsides. Clear-stemmed groves in quincunx layout were introduced, and summerhouses, belvederes and bowling pavilions were seen. Complex park networks were planted and star points cut in woods.

Three of the more extraordinary gardens of the times were Bretby, near Burton upon Trent, with its water organ that played *Lilibolaro*; Chatsworth in Derbyshire, with its cascade of 1694 devised by René Grillet; and Boughton in Northamptonshire, with several cascades.

William of Orange's accession in 1689 brought his personal standards to his gardens, principally those at Hampton Court and Kensington. His 'Dutch' taste at Hampton Court was indicated by a maze in the wilderness, urns on the east front, a tunnel arbour in the Privy Garden and an ironwork one in the Fountain Garden. William craved the greatest fountain display in Europe, while Queen Mary's obsession was her exotic plants, imported from the Netherlands and housed in 'glass cases', and her florist flowers.

William brought over his personal architect, Daniel Marot, to devise the parterre at Hampton Court, and his hand may be suspected in the wilderness at Kensington, an incredibly elaborate and no doubt costly design. In his last years William had the Fountain Garden expanded and the Privy Garden lowered twice in order that the River Thames could be seen properly. While he never achieved his fountaineering ambitions, his gardens had become among the most esteemed in Europe.

David Jacques

OPPOSITE LEFT An engraving of Cassiobury Park, Hertfordshire, by Johannes Kip and Leonard Knyff, 1707.

OPPOSITE RIGHT The Hornbeam Pergola in the recently restored Privy Gardens at Hampton Court Palace.

Aberglasney Gardens

Carmarthenshire

–

Designed for Bishop Anthony Rudd

–

c. 1600; restored 1999

–

Garden structure registered Grade II*

Aberglasney first captured the public imagination in 1999, when the BBC TV series *A Garden Lost in Time* documented the rediscovery of the structures of a cloister garden dating from the early 1600s, hidden beneath a jungle of weeds. These programmes revealed the fascinating teamwork of archaeologists and historians as they painstakingly uncovered layers of the past to trace the garden back to its origins.

In the early days of the Welsh Historic Gardens Trust, artist William Wilkins drew attention to remnants of neglected country-house gardens along the rich artery of the Tywi Valley. The Aberglasney Restoration Trust was formed to investigate the mysterious structures adjoining the semi-derelict mansion and, thanks to a generous benefactor, were able to purchase the site.

Archival research revealed that the name Aberglasney rang some cultural bells. It had been the seat of Anthony Rudd, Elizabethan Bishop of St David's 1594–1614, whose splendid tomb is in the parish church. Rudd is notorious for offending the Virgin Queen in a sermon alluding to her advancing years. In the 1720s poet John Dyer (son of the owner) sang its praises. Locally, Aberglasney chimed with myths and rumours of ghostly hauntings. Until the estate was broken up in the mid-20th century, it had prospered under neat patterns of family ownership in the 1600s, 1700s and 1800s, when wealth from church, law and empire contributed to its development.

In parallel with the historical research, archaeologists worked to remove generations of accretions around the

crumbling stone structures. They were eventually able
to date the creation of the building quite precisely to
around 1600, when such an Italianate style was popular
in fashionable gardens. Since almost every documented
example in Britain was later 'swept away' by the landscape
movement, this was a unique survival.

Much of the footage of the TV series showed hard-
hatted people working in bare earth, robbed-out trenches
and tyre-tracked mud. Often the only kind of 'plant' visible
consisted of big yellow diggers! But meanwhile future
gardening was on the agenda. It was determined that the
Cloister Garden layout should be historically appropriate,
but Penelope Hobhouse was given free rein for her design
in the relatively intact walled kitchen garden. The seeds of
Aberglasney's regeneration were being sown.

Extra pieces of the jigsaw have fitted into place. The
Trust has gradually acquired adjacent portions of the
fragmented estate to make a more cohesive entity. There
have also been some stunning innovations. While the
mansion's north and west façades have been renovated, the
ruinous central core and courtyard have been glazed over
to make an indoor garden, coined the 'Ninfarium' after the
garden of Ninfa, south of Rome.

Once the archaeologists and historians had completed
their digging, gardening could begin in earnest. With the
new century Aberglasney blossomed into one of Wales's
finest gardens. Around its historic core the place is making
history with inspired and innovative planting embracing
sound ecological principles. Today it is truly a heritage
garden of excellence, to be visited at every season.

Penny David

Bramshill House

Edward, Baron Zouche (1556–1625), an important courtier, built Bramshill House on the site of a medieval lodge and park. According to a contemporary, 'Zouche spent most of his later years at Bramshill .... Besides designing the house, he also designed the gardens.' This was not unusual, as Lord Burghley and his son, Robert Cecil, 1st Earl of Salisbury, were known to have designed their gardens at Theobalds and Hatfield House.

The house is surrounded by walled courts and gardens. To the south are the approach and entrance court (with two small angle turrets typical of many Jacobean forecourts); there is also a forecourt to the north, which provides access to the park and is flanked by walled enclosures (now formal gardens). To the west are the large walled kitchen gardens and orchards. The pleasure gardens are to the east, beneath the most important state rooms in the house. The main garden consists of a broad square platform, the width of the house, linked by a fine balustraded terrace along the garden façade. A lower garden to the south is built on a slope and was originally enclosed by walls in an unusual wedge shape (a concession to the terrain). A small pond also survives in this part of the garden; there are ponds to the south and west of the house as well.

A long tree-lined avenue extends northwards from the house to the water gardens and maze. The lake, probably intended to be square in form but with the southern side incomplete, has a large lozenge-shaped island. We know that Zouche received a bill in 1613 for £24 (quite a substantial sum) from Thomas Selby for painting 'in the

Bramshill, Hampshire

Edward, 11th Baron
Zouche
–
1605–25
–
Registered Grade I

OPPOSITE It is hoped
that the water gardens
at Bramshill will be
sensitively restored,
preserving both the
history of the gardens
and the wildlife habitat.

BELOW The garden
façade at Bramshill.

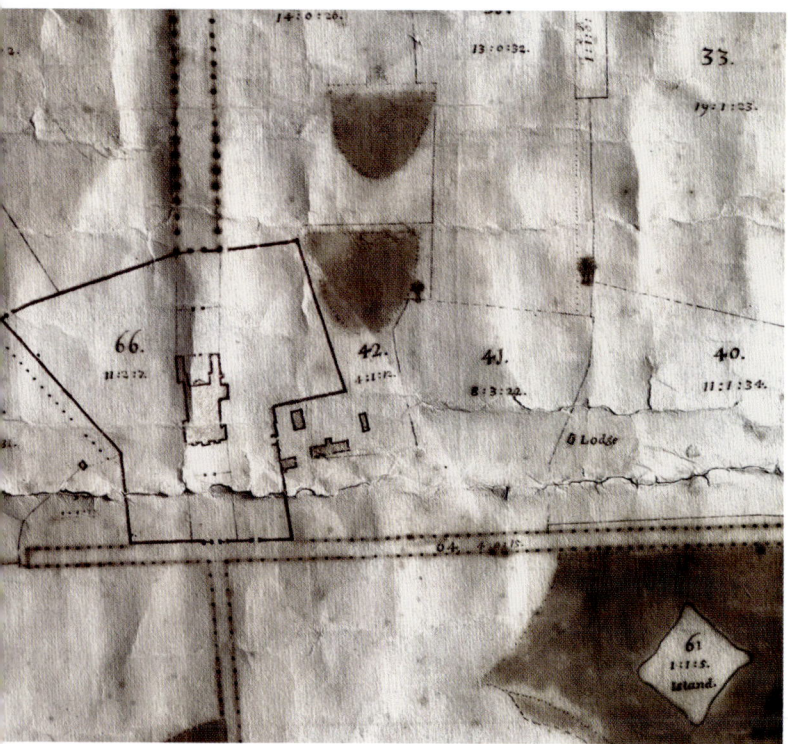

Iland'. This provides evidence that the lake was Jacobean and typical of many high-status water gardens of the period, such as those at Hatfield and Gorhambury in Hertfordshire, and Tackley in Oxfordshire. The maze was sited at the end of the avenue, but its original configuration is unclear in the 18th-century plans or surveys that survive.

What is particularly important about Bramshill is that many of the walls of the 17th-century walled gardens and forecourt survive, as do the long sculpted approach, the large lake and island, the remains of tree-lined avenues and the site of a maze. All these features appear on an important map of 1699 by Isaac Justis, probably executed when the property was purchased by the Cope family who owned it until 1935. The Copes were extremely conservative, wishing to retain the gardens in a way sympathetic to the original date of the house. Although almost all the features shown in the Justis map survive, the numerous buildings erected by the government, when the property served as the Police College (1935–2015), have drastically altered the effect of the landscape and diverted the main tree-lined avenue. It is hoped that these later features will be removed, revealing the relationship of Bramshill House and its lake, which remain the sole example of a Jacobean house and its water garden to survive together.

Paula Henderson

Oxford Botanic Garden

Rose Lane, Oxford

–

Jacob Bobart the Elder

–

1621

–

Registered Grade I

BELOW Etching of the Danby Gate in Oxford Botanic Garden, from *Old England: A Pictorial Museum of Regal, Ecclesiastical, Baronial, Municipal, and Popular Antiquities*, 1845.

When Henry Danvers, Earl of Danby, founded Oxford Physic Garden (as it was originally known) in 1621, it was the first of its kind in Britain. Danby recognized that all the best universities in Europe had their own physic gardens, the earliest being at Padua in 1545, and that they were essential for training medics and apothecaries.

Jacob Bobart the Elder (c. 1599–1680) was the first keeper of the garden. Bobart's early life is shrouded in mystery, and he is best remembered now for his supposed eccentricity, but he deserves recognition for establishing the garden's original (impressive) plant collection. He had a reputation as an auricula breeder, a fashionable plant of the day, which would have been in high demand, and which he presumably sold. He also experimented with grafting plants, and he is credited with developing a grafting method that made it possible to make the popular 'White Frontiniac' grapes bear fruit early. In 1648, Bobart compiled a catalogue of the garden's plants, which included Virginian spiderwort (*Tradescantia virginiana*) sent over from America by the younger John Tradescant, as well as other novelties like melons, which were extremely fashionable and required expert care and resources to grow successfully. A yew tree (*Taxus baccata*) planted by Bobart in 1645 still survives and can be seen in the garden today.

Jacob Bobart the Younger (1641–1719), succeeded his father as superintendent of the garden, and was crucial in its development and ongoing success. Bobart the Younger further expanded the garden's collections with plants from abroad, including American aloes, Indian figs, African

OPPOSITE The garden continues its legacy by laying out taxonomic and medicinal beds, as can be seen in the walled garden.

BELOW RIGHT This view, facing north, looks now much as it would have done to the Bobarts.

RIGHT The gateway in the South wall was added in the 18th century, when the site was expanded into what is today known as the lower garden.

geraniums, cedars and black walnuts from Virginia, among many others. In 'Vertumnus', the poem Abel Evans dedicated to Bobart the Younger in 1713, the reader is told not only of Bobart's care of the garden, but also of his continuing efforts to collect and collate specimens for his 'hortus siccus' (herbarium), which is 'With utmost Diligence amass'd, / And shall as many Ages last.' His herbarium remains in the university's collections and has been extremely valuable for botanists and historians alike.

The garden continued to expand its collections and attain tropical plants for its hothouses through the 18th and 19th centuries. Additionally, by the 20th century, the garden had become a source of inspiration for several authors, including Lewis Carroll and Oscar Wilde, and more recently it has featured in Philip Pullman's *His Dark Materials* (1995–2000). J.R.R. Tolkien was inspired by the garden, particularly its black pine tree, which supposedly inspired the Ents in *The Lord of the Rings* (1954).

The garden has had many distinguished visitors over its 400-year history, including royalty. Most notably, Cosimo III de' Medici (1642–1723) visited in 1669 and William of Orange (1650–1702) in 1670. More recently, HRH King Charles III, who is patron of the garden, visited in 2021 and planted a tree which was grown from a seed of Tolkien's black pine.

With several ongoing restoration, research and conservation projects in the works, the garden continues to celebrate its heritage alongside developing its impressive plant collection and generating new botanical knowledge.

India Cole

Drummond Castle Gardens

The early Victorian, formal terraced garden at Drummond Castle is the best of its type in Scotland and of European significance. It is designated as outstanding in Historic Environment Scotland's Inventory of Gardens and Designed Landscapes.

The 5-hectare (12-acre) garden overlays a much older foundation adjoining the ancient 15th-century stronghold of the distinguished Drummond family, Earls of Perth. Between 1630 and 1636, the 2nd Earl created a formal terraced garden, of which the remarkable obelisk sundial is a survival. It was not until the 1820s and 1830s that major reshaping of the garden and terracing was undertaken in 'antique' Renaissance style. The force behind this work was Clementina Sarah Drummond and her husband Peter Robert Burrell, Lord Willoughby, later 22nd Baron Willoughby de Eresby. The layout and planting are attributed to notable landscape designer and plantsman, Lewis Kennedy, son of John Kennedy of Vineyard Nursery, Hammersmith. George Penrose Kennedy, Lewis's son and a pupil of Charles Barry, also had a hand in the work.

Of note is the long avenue of beech leading to the castle garden. This was revived and replanted for Queen Victoria's three-day visit to Drummond, in September 1842.

The garden was carefully maintained into the 20th century. In the early 1950s, Nancy Phyllis Astor and her husband, the 3rd Earl of Ancaster simplified the dense evergreen planting while retaining the main components. Since 1978, the garden has been under the care of the Grimsthorpe and Drummond Castle Trust.

Perthshire
–
Earlier periods warrant further research; Lewis Kennedy and George Penrose Kennedy
–
1630–36; 1820s–1830s
–
Designated Category A

RIGHT The 17th-century obelisk sundial commissioned by John Drummond, 2nd Earl of Perth.

OPPOSITE A small section of the lower parterre from the terracing.

The view south from the terracing is unforgettable. Quintessentially Scottish, the garden is stylistically French and Italian with a hint of Medici. The fine terracing, dramatic central vista, immaculate topiary, yew and box hedging, the water features and the many architectural embellishments in combination with seasonal planting, create a dramatic effect. The family heraldry is depicted in the box-edged planting and in wavy bands of pebbles around the unique obelisk sundial, the central focus of the Saltire parterre.

Conservation of the extensive box hedging is critical to the design. Where it has been affected by blight, it is now being replaced by a new 'heritage' blight-resistant variety, recommended by the European Boxwood and Topiary Society. Cultivation of the Kitchen Garden is much reduced, but a small Scottish-heritage-apple orchard was planted about 12 years ago, to propagate 19th-century varieties including 'Tower of Glamis' and 'Golden Hornet'.

The extensive work on conserving and maintaining this outstanding work of art is ever demanding. Major restoration of the obelisk sundial was completed in 2019. Since 2020, several volunteers have become involved in supporting the eight permanent garden staff, and a record and plan of current garden planting has been made. The mansion remains a private residence, but the garden is open to the public from May to October.

Fiona Jamieson

Jardin de Vuillton, Construict Par tres noble et tres puissant Seigneur PHILIPPE COMTE DE PENBROOKE ET MONGOMERI Baron horbert de Cardif, Seigneur parr et Rose de Candall, Narmion, S.t ques inland, gardien de lestanerie aux Contez de Cornuall et deuon Chamberlain de la Maison du Roy, Chevalier du tres noble ordre de la Jartiere Lieutenant general pour le Roy aux prouinces de Vuillts Jom ceilles du Concell Priue' de sa Majesti'e Isaac de caus Inuent

Wilton Garden

Wilton, Wiltshire

–

**Isaac de Caus, advised
by Inigo Jones**

–

c. 1632–42

–

Registered Grade I

LEFT Marble relief of
Galatea from the grotto,
c. 1635, now in the Italian
Garden.

OPPOSITE Engraved
bird's-eye view of Wilton
Garden by Isaac de Caus,
c. 1645.

The formal garden at Wilton was created for Philip Herbert, 4th Earl of Pembroke (1584-1650), courtier and friend to Charles I and fellow lover of the arts. Although long gone, the garden was extremely well-recorded in drawings, engravings, paintings and visitors' accounts and many pieces of its sculpture, statuary and architecture survive. It was one of the greatest of Caroline gardens.

Pembroke inherited the estate in 1630 and asked Inigo Jones, the royal architect, to draw up plans for a new house and garden. Jones was busy elsewhere so Isaac de Caus, a hydraulic engineer from Dieppe, was delegated to take over, advised by Jones. His drawings and the set of engravings published in *Wilton Garden*, give a vivid impression of its design, sculpture and wonderful waterworks, all inspired by Jones's knowledge of the theatre and Italian and French ideas.

The large walled area (about 4 hectares/9½ acres) stretched from the house across the River Nadder and beyond. It had a broad central walk and was divided into three sections. Next to the house were embroidered parterres containing four fountains with female figures from classical mythology and history. Some of the plinths have been reused and three marble statues are kept in the house.

In the middle section were two groves of trees or 'wildernesses', each with a large statue in the centre. Beyond were pools with fountains in the form of fountain-columns surmounted by golden crowns rotated by the spouting water. The statues of Bacchus and Flora, once in the groves, now adorn a bridge in the grounds, and one of

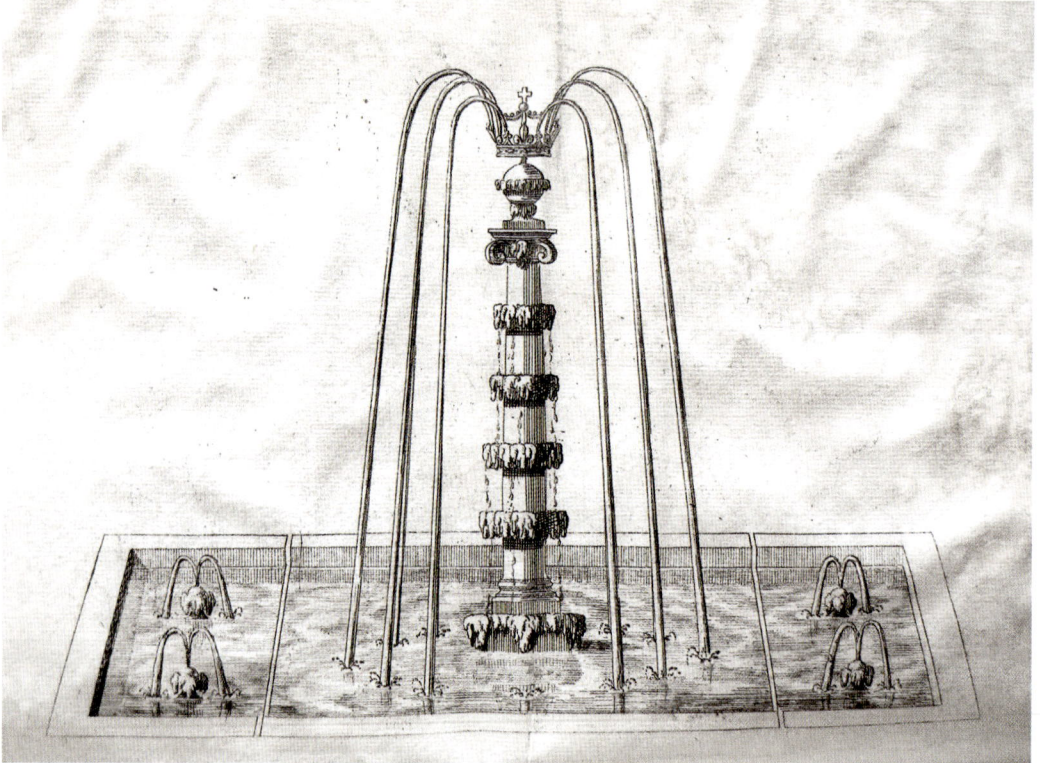

ABOVE LEFT Marble figure of Bacchus carrying Cupid from the Wilderness, c. 1635, now on the Image Bridge in the grounds.

ABOVE RIGHT Detail of a engraving of Bacchus carrying Cupid from *Wilton Garden*, c. 1645.

LEFT 'A fountain surmounted with a Crown', engraving from *Wilton Garden*.

OPPOSITE A surviving column fountain.

the columns also survives. A much-discussed feature here was the River Nadder, winding through the groves. It could have been straightened or diverted but instead this single asymmetrical element was retained. It has been argued that it was a deliberate reference to the pastoral romance *Arcadia*, written at Wilton in 1580 by Philip Sidney, Pembroke's uncle, which probably inspired much of the iconography in the garden.

The third section took the form of a cherry orchard, with a brass copy by Hubert Le Sueur of a famous Roman antiquity – the Borghese Gladiator – in its central oval. This was later given to Sir Robert Walpole.

At the end of the garden was its most memorable feature – a grotto. Its inner walls were ornamented with marble reliefs on the classical themes of Europa and Galatea, and it contained complex waterworks, which could spray the visitor, reproduce the song of nightingales and create a 'fountain of the three rainbows' – perhaps with the ingenious use of mirrors. The secret of its operation was said to have died with De Caus, its inventor. Parts of the grotto migrated round the garden and now decorate a building in the grounds, while the reliefs (by Nicholas Stone and his workshop, like nearly all the sculpture) are in a private garden near the house.

Wilton garden was already somewhat neglected when Celia Fiennes visited in 1685, and was replaced in the 1730s by the landscape garden with its Palladian Bridge, which has become even more famous than its forebear.

Sally Jeffery

Ham House

The Countess of Dysart's garden at Ham is an outstanding surviving example of a late 17th-century garden with a sequence of original walled enclosures.

Ham House was built on the banks of the River Thames near Richmond in 1610. Its early walled gardens were extended and redesigned for Elizabeth Murray, 2nd Countess of Dysart, and her husband John Maitland, 1st Duke of Lauderdale, after their marriage in 1672. Elizabeth lived there until her death in 1698.

The plan of the garden was axial and symmetrical. A large terrace ran the length of the house to the south, where in the summer the most prized plants could be displayed. Aviaries for singing birds were attached to the bay windows, with scented jasmines growing nearby. From the terrace, you could descend some steps to an open area with a broad central gravel path. Plain plats of scythed grass on each side were divided into quarters, each displaying a sculpture in the centre. Beyond was a wilderness or grove of trees where radiating walks bordered with clipped hedges led to an oval grassed central area. Within the divisions were winding paths and small summerhouses or alcoves, offering both privacy and a place for entertainment. The design of the grove was inspired by the most recent innovations in French gardens, which Elizabeth would have known from publications, and had probably seen on her visits to France. She employed two French gardeners – Jacques Chesneau and John Flaigmell – who no doubt added to the skills of their English colleagues in caring for the exotics.

Richmond, Greater London

-

Designed for the Countess of Dysart

-

1610; extended 1672–98

-

Registered Grade I

OPPOSITE The entrance to the Wilderness.

BELOW Ham House from the south, attributed to Hendrick Danckerts, c. 1675–79.

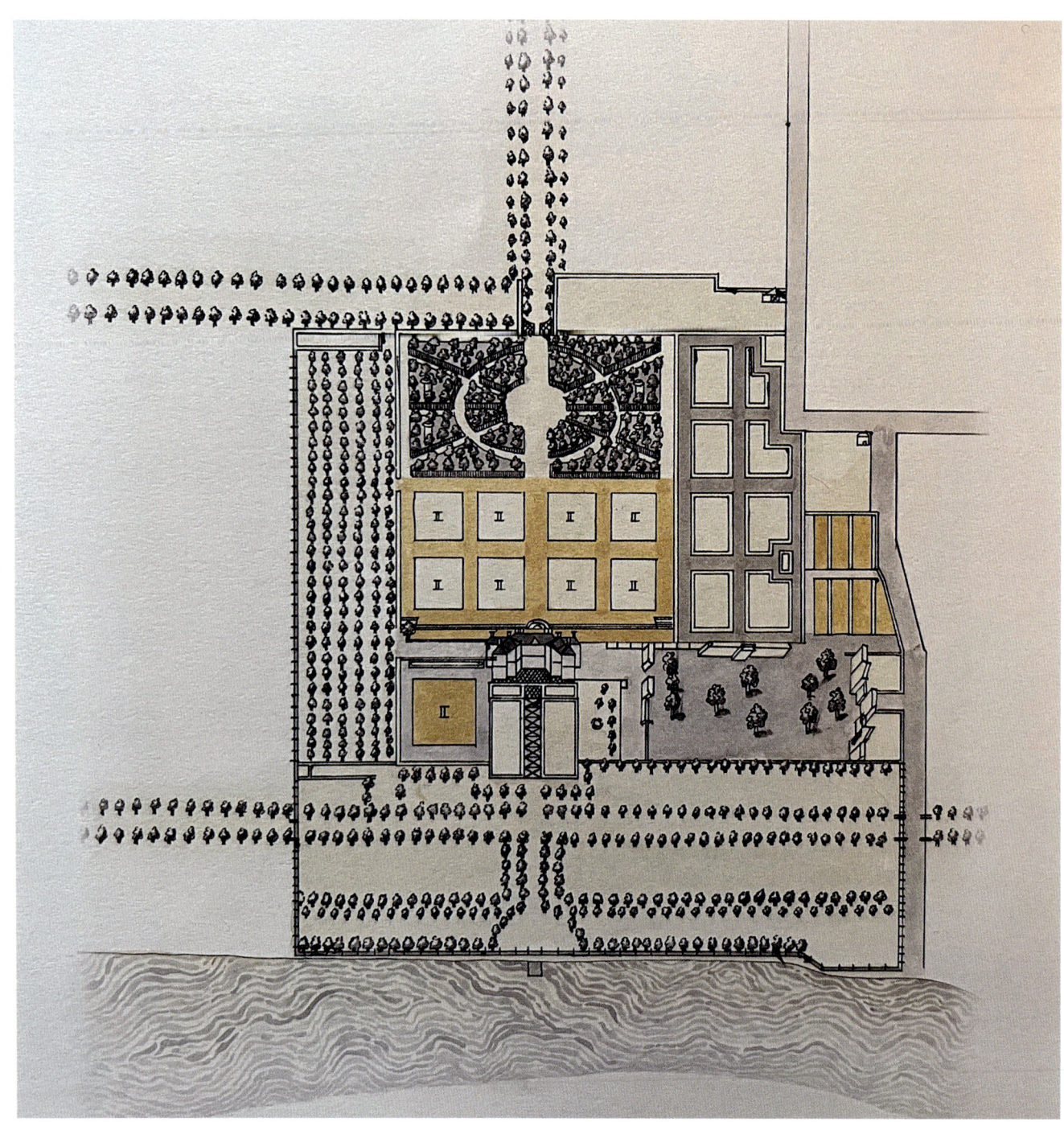

On one side of the main garden lay a regular wooded area, while on the other was a large productive kitchen garden with a greenhouse or orangery at one end, in which tender plants could be overwintered. This building, like the house itself, featured windows with secondary glazing – an innovative idea to give extra protection from the cold weather. Elizabeth was interested in exotics such as orange and lemon trees, which were particularly appreciated for their evergreen leaves, scented flowers and attractive fruit. She also grew myrtles (*Myrtus communis*), oleanders (*Nerium oleander*) and pomegranates (*Punica granatum*). Among her most prized plants were tuberoses (*Polianthes tuberosa*). These had tuberous roots and flowers rather like hyacinths and were heavily scented. Originating in Mexico, they had become fashionable in French gardens such as Versailles but required careful cultivation and protection. Records show 200 were purchased for Ham in 1682.

Fruit trees were grown on all the walls. Cherries were particularly popular, with 395 listed in an inventory of 1653. These were a feature of a small private flower garden on the east side of the house which Elizabeth could reach from a door in her closet.

Ham was owned by the descendants of the Duke and Countess until 1948 when it was donated to the National Trust. Although the original planting was removed in the 18th century, the walled divisions remained and the arrangement of c. 1670 was recreated for the National Trust in the 1970s, based on contemporary records and plans.

Sally Jeffery

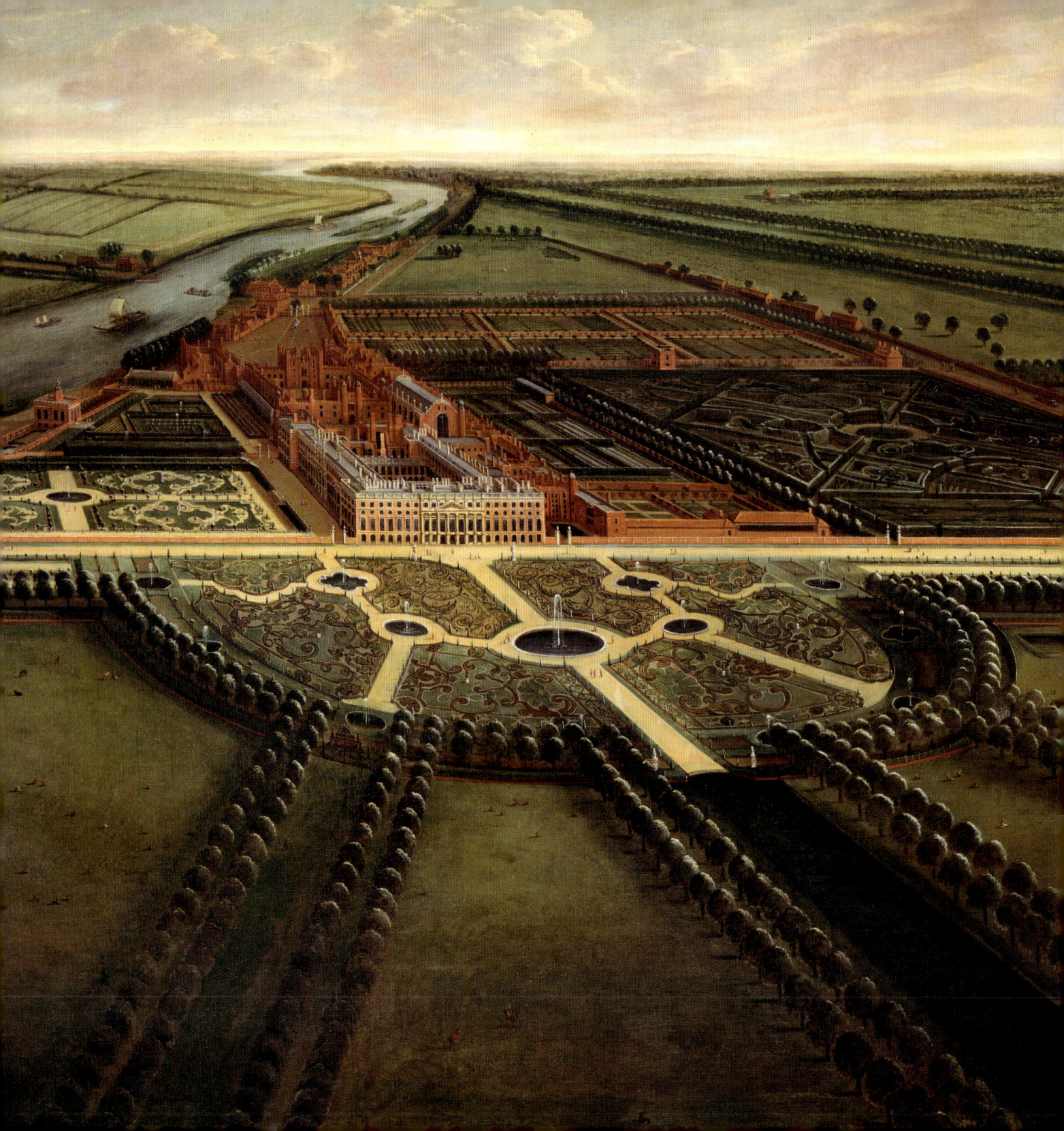

Hampton Court

OPPOSITE Bird's-eye view of Hampton Court from the east by Johannes Kip, c. 1707.

BELOW One of the Tudor 'ponds' with original walling except to the right where William III's Privy Garden wall has encroached.

Greater London

–

Adrian May, George London, Daniel Marot and others

–

1520s–1712

–

Registered Grade I

Hampton Court's gardens have been famous since Cardinal Wolsey first created a two-storey gallery, knot gardens and an ornamental orchard within the moat. In 1529 he presented it to Henry VIII who greatly enlarged it, first by setting out a tiltyard with towers and a Great Orchard between the moat and park wall. Then, in 1535, he added the New Garden; the Privy Garden, a huge mount topped with a banqueting house; and the Pond Yard. The surrounding Great Wall was battlemented, the first of several mock-fortified gardens.

In 1583 French specialist John Markye reformed the Privy Garden with a chequerboard of red brick dust, white sand and green grass, and hedgework surmounted by figurative box topiary. Over time fountains in the form of obelisks embellished the knots, and the gardens were decorated with sundials.

A bowling green alongside the Privy Garden was created in 1636 and the 'Longford River' dug in 1638 intended to supply water features which had to be abandoned at the Civil War. Hampton Court survived as Oliver Cromwell's official residence. He acquired the Arethusa fountain from Somerset House and other statues for the Privy Garden in the mid-1650s, implying that it had been converted to the fashion for plain grass and gravel.

At the Restoration in 1660, Adrian May created the Long Water across the House Park – briefly the longest in Europe – flanked by avenues of imported lime trees. The mile-long quadruple Great Avenue was planted across the Hare Warren (today Bushy Park) in 1664.

When in 1689 Parliament voted huge sums to convert Hampton Court into a major European palace for William III, the Great Orchard became the Wilderness with its maze. His head gardener was George London, but he brought in his Dutch gardens team, and personal architect, Daniel Marot. Marot's greatest design was the Fountain Garden, a parterre of *broderie* and cutwork intended to have 13 fountains, enclosed within ironwork gates, rails and decorative panels by Jean Tijou. Radial avenues were inserted into the 30-year-old half-moon. Queen Mary took charge of the gardens to the south, adding 'Glass cases' to house her tropical exotics, and displaying orange trees in the Pond Yard. The Privy Garden became a huge flower garden.

A basin and horse chestnuts were added to the Great Avenue in 1699 and William Talman further enlarged the Fountain Garden. The Privy Garden was lowered for a view of the river, and the spoil made into a terrace along the river leading to a new bowling green. A scrollwork parterre was set between side terraces, one with the arbour, as depicted by Leonard Knyff and Johannes Kip.

Queen Anne remade the parterre in 1707, and surrounded the Fountain Garden with canals and incorporated them into the area. George I and II, and Lancelot 'Capability' Brown, chief gardener 1764–83, maintained the gardens as found. The later fashion for naturalistic gardens meant Hampton Court became derided, but tourists came to see the maze, vine and yews.

A survey in 1981 led to conservation projects, including replanting avenues, and the Privy Garden was restored in 1995 after a fire in the State Apartments.

David Jacques

ABOVE An Edwardian restoration of a Henry VIII pond and later Queen Mary's 'auricula garden'.

OPPOSITE Oblique view of the Privy Garden as restored 1993–95 to how it was in Queen Anne's reign.

Chatsworth

Chatsworth is unique in that it evidences garden and park-making by one family over 500 years. Sir William Cavendish bought the manor in 1549 and built a new house after marrying Bess of Hardwick. In 1560 he created a garden on a levelled area sown with herbs and flowers. By 1617 their son Thomas, 1st Earl of Devonshire, recorded a large estate with a park and gardens, an orchard and areas for deer hunting.

William Cavendish, the 4th Earl/1st Duke of Devonshire (1641-1707), transformed the gardens to demonstrate his allegiance to William III and the Glorious Revolution. In 1688 came the West Parterre, featuring quarters with grass cutwork, surrounded by lavender-edged borders and shaped trees, designed by George London. The Great Parterre implemented in 1694 was also commissioned from London and Henry Wise. A new greenhouse was built, and a temple dedicated to Flora, wildernesses and a grove with a circular pond with copper weeping willow fountain as a centre piece (1693-95). There were further waterworks and a cascade created by Grillet in 1694-96, and in 1702-3 a cascade house by Thomas Archer and the great canal pond.

William Kent's sketches in the 1740s envisioned a less ordered design and although this was not implemented, the parterres were removed, preparing the ground metaphorically for Lancelot 'Capability' Brown. From 1760-64 Brown created a new park to the west, with a curvaceous new drive that approached the house at the northern end, requiring two new bridges, designed by James Paine. The terracing was removed to create a grass slope and a kitchen garden appeared to the south-west.

Bakewell, Derbyshire
-
George London
and Henry Wise;
Capability Brown;
Joseph Paxton
-
1560-onwards
-
Registered Grade I

RIGHT The Cascade was built by the French engineer Grillet in 1696. It was extended five years later, and a Cascade House added by Thomas Archer in 1702-3.

ABOVE The 1st Duke's greenhouse (1698) moved and altered in the 19th century by Joseph Paxton.

LEFT The serpentine beech hedge planted in 1953.

OPPOSITE The Canal Pond, created in 1702, with the Emperor Fountain of 1844.

The 6th Duke inherited the estate in 1811 and later appointed the ambitious Joseph Paxton as head gardener, who inspired the duke to start plant collecting, which required horticultural innovations. These included the Great Conservatory (1840) – the largest horticultural structure built to date – orchid houses and a lily house for the Amazon waterlily (*Victoria amazonica*). Outdoors, collections of woody plants were included in the Arboretum and Pinetum. The waterworks were renewed and in 1844 the Emperor Fountain – the highest gravity fed fountain in the world – was created for an expected visit by the Russian Emperor.

After the First World War the lack of resources for maintaining the gardens led to the demolition of the Great Conservatory. After inheriting the estate in 1950, the 11th Duke and Duchess embarked on a new stage in its development, carefully simplifying and embellishing the estate, without damaging the intricate qualities of its layout. Two rows of pleached lime trees were planted to the west front in 1952, serpentine hedges in 1953 and a maze within the base of the Great Conservatory in 1962. A modern greenhouse was added in 1970, a cottage garden in 1989 and a new kitchen garden north of the stables in 1994.

Soon after the 12th Duke inherited the estate in 2004, he launched The Masterplan, which included clearing out overgrown vegetation and Victorian planting, and commissioning new designs by fashionable designers including Dan Pearson and Tom Stuart-Smith. The estate now hosts large-scale events, including horse trials, as well as workshops, modern sculpture exhibitions and more.

Jan Woudstra

Powis Castle

The garden of Powis Castle is one of the most spectacular and historically important gardens in Britain. Its dramatic, brick-built terraces drop steeply down the side of a gritstone ridge overlooking the Severn Valley. The castle towers above. This formal garden is the epitome of late 17th-century baroque formality. It is a rare and well-preserved example of a style that went rapidly out of fashion in the following century.

The garden is the result of several major phases of development. It is dominated by the terraces, built by the 1st and 2nd marquesses of Powis in the last decade of the 17th century. Their architect was probably William Winde, who also created the formal garden at Cliveden, Berkshire. It is no coincidence that the terraces bear a strong resemblance to those of the French royal palace of St Germain-en-Laye, Paris, where William Herbert, the 1st Marquess (1626–96), a Catholic, lived in exile during this period.

There were originally six long terraces, now four. A striking feature of the garden is the row of huge, clipped yews, known as 'tumps', along the top terrace, planted by the 2nd Marquess in the 1720s. The middle of the second terrace is backed by an arcaded aviary. Four lead statues of shepherds and shepherdesses, by John van Nost, stood on the balustrade. No longer – they were stolen in January 1992. At the back of the third terrace is an orangery, whose windows and doors were added in the early 20th century. The fine lead statue of a peacock came from Claremont, Surrey. The fourth terrace has a slope below, originally terraced and planted with fruit trees. A large, formal garden,

Welshpool, Powys
–
Probably William Winde; William Emes
–
1690 onwards
–
Registered Grade I

RIGHT Yew 'tumps' on the top terrace at Powis, planted in the 1720s, with Aviary Terrace below.

BELOW The former kitchen garden became an ornamental garden in the early 20th century.

OPPOSITE A view of the park, originally laid out by William Emes in the 18th century.

with fountains and other waterworks, was created in the valley floor below at the beginning of the 18th century.

By the second half of the 18th century the formal gardens seemed very old-fashioned. The designer William Emes was employed by Henry Herbert, the 1st Earl of Powis, to bring them up to date. He proposed dynamiting the terraces, which mercifully didn't happen. Instead they were neglected and the clipped formal yews allowed to grow out. The water garden was removed, its statues redistributed around the garden, and the ridge on the south edge of the garden, called the Wilderness, was planted informally. Some of the oaks Emes planted here survive.

The garden's present-day exuberant, colourful planting owes its existence to Lady Violet, wife of George Herbert,

4th Earl of Powis, who transformed the garden between 1911 and 1929. Her most radical step was to remove the kitchen garden from its position near the terraces to a more distant one, following a gale in 1912, which blew down the elms that screened it. Violet did not like 'the repulsive sight of the detestable little [hot] houses ....' The garden became ornamental. She also criticized architect G.F. Bodley's attempt to convert the statue of Fame into a fountain: 'The horse looked as if it was trying to jump out of a footbath ....' Powis Castle and its garden were bequeathed to the National Trust in 1952.

Elisabeth Whittle

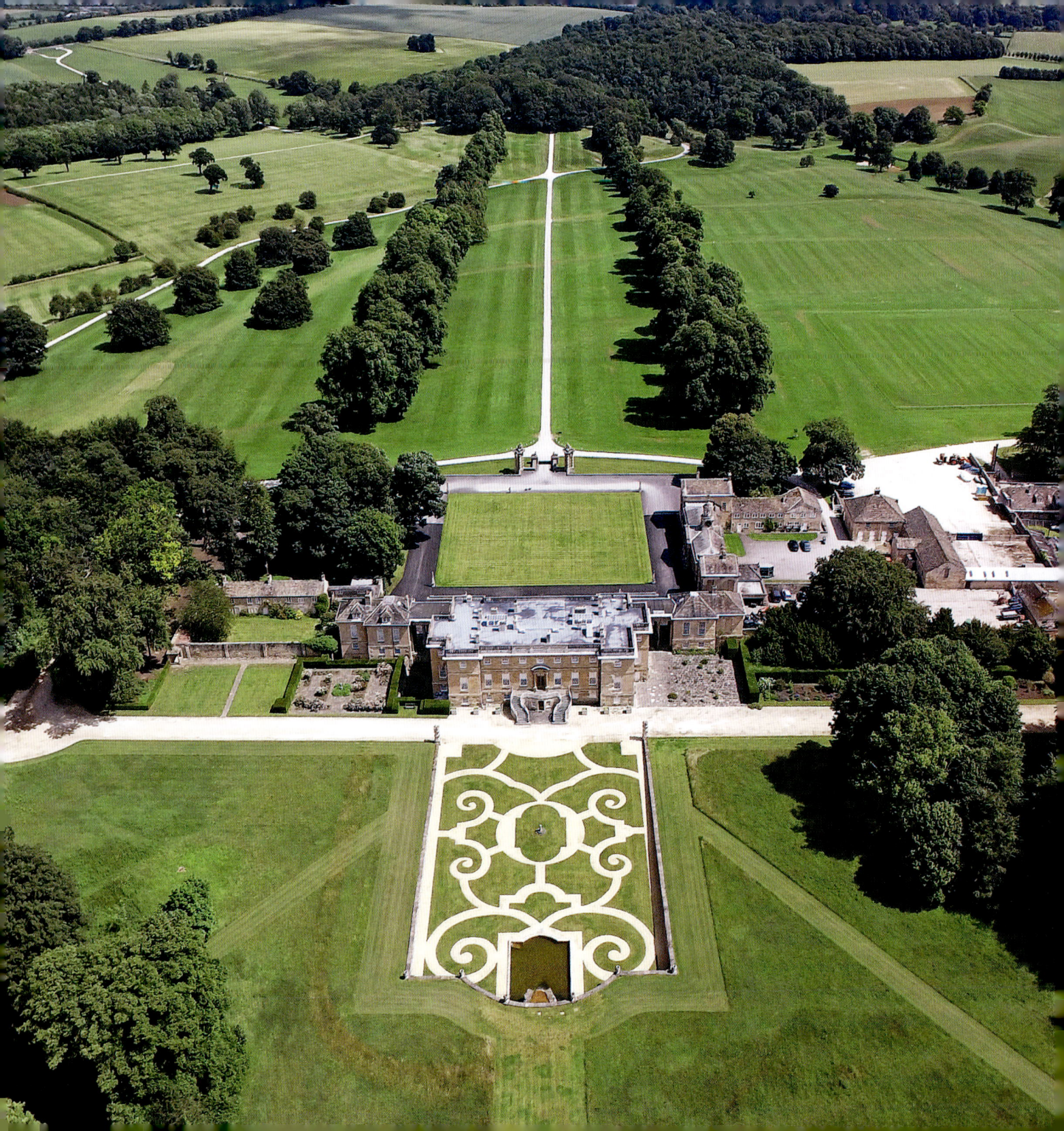

Bramham Park

Bramham, Yorkshire

-

Robert Benson

-

1698–1731

-

Registered Grade I

'If ever house and gardens must be regarded as one ensemble, it is here. Bramham is a grand and unusual house, but its gardens are grander and even more unusual.'
NIKOLAUS PEVSNER, THE BUILDINGS OF ENGLAND

OPPOSITE An aerial view of the house and driveway at Bramham Park, showing the Parterre Garden, axially aligned with the house.

BELOW Bramham Park by J.F. Neale, 1818.

The story of Bramham begins in 1693 when 17-year-old Robert Benson was sent off on the Grand Tour. He came back full of ideas about Italian architecture and French garden design which he slowly proceeded to put into practice until his death in 1731. His daughter Harriet and her husband George Fox continued to ornament the estate with many garden buildings, including several by James Paine. After that, time largely stood still. The house itself is an extraordinary survival; a fire swept through it in 1828 rendering it uninhabitable, and it was finally rebuilt in 1908 by Detmar Blow.

Most of the parkland, although highly geometric in layout, is not axially aligned with the mansion. The Parterre Garden directly in front is the exception. Its level ground is cut into the hillside, and backed with a stone wall complete with a fountain, which was once fed with water via a cascade down the hill behind.

Instead, the main garden axis – the Broadwalk – runs at right angles to the house. At one end, close to the house, is the Chapel, repurposed from an orangery. From there a long, beech-hedged *allée* leads into the wooded parkland, meeting up with others to skirt the perimeter and passing an array of urns and statues and a Tuscan Temple. In the other direction the Broadwalk stretches deceptively into the

far distance, ending with an obelisk on a wooded hilltop, but changes in ground level conceal how Bramham revels in water.

First, a magnificent series of stone pools with dragon's-head fountains and cascades step down the hillside into a deep, almost hidden valley. Set well back to one side from the uppermost pool, is an octagonal Gothic Temple based on a design of Batty Langley, and beyond that is the T-Pond. This is a long canal dug out in the 1720s, which joins, at an unusual angle, another wider, rectangular pond. It is a good example of the Roman poet Horace's desire for things to be *dulce et utile*, both beautiful and useful. Not only does the water reflect the sky and its surroundings like a mirror, but more practically it acts as a reservoir for the pools and stone cascades, including the one in the Parterre Garden.

Crossing the valley, the Broadwalk arrives at a rotunda which sits atop a deep, stone-lined ha-ha, and was perhaps inspired by William Kent's Temple of Ancient Virtue at Stowe (1737). Behind it, at the centre of a series of woodland rides is the obelisk erected in memory of Harriet's only son, which forms the final stop on the vista from the house.

Virtually unchanged since its creation, in *The Gardens of England* (1907) Charles Holmes described Bramham as 'a unique example of garden-making; there is no other place of the same character in England.'

David Marsh

GARDENS IN THE 18ᵗʰ CENTURY

The 18th century is often described as a period that saw a steady progression from highly artificial, geometric and enclosed gardens, towards more 'naturalistic' designs, culminating in the sweeping, irregular parklands of Lancelot 'Capability' Brown. But while there is much truth in this simple story, it needs to be treated with caution. The taste for regularity and geometry declined only slowly, even in the grounds of the most fashionable residences. And there was no simple succession of styles through the century, but rather a complex pattern of overlapping and at times parallel approaches to garden and landscape design.

By 1720, complex parterres had generally been replaced in the gardens of the social elite by neatly trimmed 'plats' or lawns. But avenues, topiary, straight gravel paths, geometric water bodies ('canals' and 'basins') and 'wildernesses' – that is, areas of ornamental woodland dissected by hedged paths – all remained popular, with the latter often coming to occupy much of the garden area. Designs were simple, sometimes sparse, but they were still essentially geometric. Sculptures provided focal points, and while flowering shrubs were important features, floral displays tended to be concentrated in a special flower garden.

Through the 1720s and 1730s landscape designers took this repertoire of features and used it in new ways. They created simplified geometric landscapes laid out on a large scale, and in which temples and other classical structures played an increasingly important role. Established elements took on exciting new forms. The wildernesses of the early 18th century expanded into 'forest gardens', dissected by straight *allées* focused on classical buildings, as at St Paul's Walden Bury in Hertfordshire, where the design was cut out of a pre-existing area of ancient, semi-natural woodland.

LEFT *A Perspective View of the Bowling Green &c. at Gubbins in Hertfordshire,* Jean B.C. Chatelain, c. 1750.

OPPOSITE Looking towards the Temple of Apollo at Stourhead, Wiltshire.

Basins and canals swelled into rather stiff, semi-geometric lakes, like that created at Blenheim in Oxfordshire in the 1720s. Above all, designs were more closely attuned to the natural topography, in part to achieve dramatic effect and in part, once again, as a consequence of their often grand scale.

Sir John Vanbrugh pioneered this new approach at Blenheim before 1710, and subsequently at Castle Howard in North Yorkshire, but Charles Bridgeman was the most important and prolific designer in this period. He paid particular attention to the 'genius of the place', frequently aligning some of the major axes in a design with the principal features of the natural topography – ridges, valleys – rather than arranging everything at right angles to, or parallel with, the principal façades of the mansion. At the same time, he was happy to make more local modifications to landforms, involving extensive schemes of earth movement. Indeed, Bridgeman was a veritable sculptor of earth. His designs regularly featured grassed terraces, amphitheatres, and ha-has or 'sunken fences' flanked by raised walks, which were sometimes provided with semi-circular, bastion-like projections, reminiscent of contemporary military fortifications. The latter, in particular, were widely adopted by garden designers, with good examples surviving at Bramham in West Yorkshire. Such arrangements allowed visitors to 'command' the prospect, and in general gardens became more outward looking, providing views across the surrounding countryside or, more usually, over an adjacent deer park, a feature which remained, as in earlier centuries, an indispensable adjunct of the elite residence. Here avenues might be planted, albeit more sparsely than in earlier periods, although sometimes the principal vistas were more subtly framed by geometric plantations, as, for example, at Houghton in Norfolk, the home of Sir Robert Walpole.

Designs became both more outward looking, and less firmly tied to the geometry of the house, in another way. Bridgeman and other designers often provided carriage drives leading through the park to some elevated viewpoint, as at Tring in Hertfordshire; or created extensive and complex gardens, which lay at a distance from the house and invisible from it, in order to exploit some particular topographic opportunity. At Gobions, also in Hertfordshire, Bridgeman designed a garden of walks and clearings cut through existing woodland to either side of a deeply incised valley, some 250 metres (275 yards) to the south of Gobions house and quite separate from it. Typically, classical sculptures and temples formed focal points in the design.

Well into the 1740s, most fashionable gardens were laid out in this expansive but simplified geometric style, which developed in a complex range of ways. Of particular note is the great formal water garden, with its geometric pools and temples, created by John Aislabie at Studley Royal in North Yorkshire between 1725 and 1742. But here, as at a number of other places, geometric structure was becoming subservient to the irregular character of the natural landforms, and from around 1730 William Kent, originally a painter and architect, began to create gardens characterized by serpentine more than straight lines. Gently winding paths, forming circuits, led past shrubberies, through woodland and across lawns irregularly planted with trees. In the wider landscape, ovoid clumps were planted within the parkland and crowned the summits of distant hills. Temples, and classical structures like obelisks, were particularly prominent features, and lakes became more serpentine and natural-looking. Kent's designs in many ways resembled three-dimensional versions of the idealized representations of Italian scenery painted by the artist Claude Lorrain, which were immensely popular with wealthy individuals accustomed to undertaking the Grand Tour, and who were often busy building Palladian mansions loosely modelled on Italian villas. But it is important to emphasize that Kent's serpentine designs still usually co-existed with, or incorporated, strongly geometric features, as for example at Holkham in Norfolk or, on a more intimate scale, Rousham in Oxfordshire. At Stowe in Buckinghamshire the lawns, temples and irregular planting of his famous Elysian Fields lay within a wider geometric landscape featuring avenues, straight gravel paths and linear vistas, designed by Bridgeman. Kent's garden here was a discrete experience, with buildings and features carefully laid out to convey the political and philosophical views of its owner, Richard Temple, 1st Viscount Cobham.

Modern scholars have detected subtle philosophical meanings in other gardens laid out, in the middle of the century, in this serpentine style, including Stourhead in Wiltshire. But many such interpretations are unconvincing and gardens at this time generally appealed more to the emotions than the intellect. The buildings at Stowe were not all classical – they included the Gothic Temple designed by James Gibbs in the early 1740s – and in many gardens the middle decades of the century saw a steady proliferation in both the styles, and the numbers, of ornamental buildings. Classical temples were joined by Chinese pagodas and bridges, by gothic ruins and Muslim mosques, by hermitages (sometimes complete with resident hermit), 'root houses', cascades and 'Turkish tents', often placed in close proximity. All were set within areas of irregular planting using the latest shrubs acquired from remote lands. In 1752 the Earl of Shaftesbury's gardens at Wimborne St Giles in Dorset featured a cascade, a 'thatch'd house', a 'round pavilion' on a mount, 'Shake Spear's House, in which there is a small statue of him', a pavilion and both a stone bridge and a 'Chinese Bridge'. Later changes have usually made these gardens less cluttered and more refined. At Stourhead the surviving structures scattered around the lake – the classical Pantheon, Grotto, Temples of Flora and Apollo, the Five Arched Bridge and the genuinely medieval St Peter's Pump, brought from Bristol – were originally accompanied by a more diverse range, including a Turkish Tent, Chinese Pavilion, Gothic Greenhouse, Chinese Bridge and Venetian Seat (the mosque planned for an island in the lake was never built). Such gardens were designed to stir the emotions: to evoke thoughts of distant countries, reactions of surprise, melancholy or delight. They were places to have fun.

There was much variety in this exuberant, mid-century period of design. Some gardens were primarily intended for the private enjoyment of owners and guests. Others were regularly opened to 'polite' visitors, who might attend in vast numbers. One noteworthy variant was the *ferme ornée*, or ornamented farm, notable examples of which were created by William Shenstone at the Leasowes in Warwickshire and Philip Southcote at Wooburn in Surrey. In these, serpentine paths, shrubberies, sculptures and buildings were set within

ABOVE The Elysian Fields and Temple of Ancient Virtue at Stowe, Buckinghamshire.

fields and farmland, normal landscapes of agricultural production. Whatever their precise form, fashionable gardens displayed rather stiffly serpentine lines, often contained a jumble of buildings, and continued to boast structured, formal elements, including straight gravel walks, avenues, linear vistas and geometric water bodies.

'Capability' Brown's earliest designs were in this tradition – rather cluttered, and combining somewhat mannered serpentine features with simplified geometric ones. He began his career working as Clerk of Works at Stowe. But soon after setting up as an independent designer in 1750 he was creating landscapes in a different, simpler style. The house was now set within an extensive, open expanse of turf, scattered in an irregular and fairly sparse manner with individual trees and clumps of woodland, and surrounded in whole or part by a perimeter belt. Where possible, such 'landscape parks' boasted a serpentine lake, and most contained only a small number of ornamental, usually classical, structures and buildings. In effect, Brown took the traditional landscape of the deer park – grass and scattered trees – gave it a more manicured appearance, merged it with elements of the 'serpentine' garden and made it the principal setting for the mansion. To protect clumps and free-standing trees, deer were often banished, to be replaced by sheep and cattle. Straight lines were everywhere replaced by curves and sinuosity: avenues now disappeared and in their place serpentine drives and rides ran across the parkland and through perimeter belts, forming one or more extended circuits to be enjoyed from a carriage or on horseback. Walled enclosures were removed from around the house but gardens did not of course disappear. 'Pleasure grounds' featuring lawns, specimen trees, serpentine paths, shrubberies, flowers and often a flower garden, remained. They were divided from the park by a ha-ha more discrete than those of earlier times, so that the two merged visually. Viewed from the park, and from the approach drive running through it, the mansion appeared to stand alone, 'free of walls', within the open parkland.

Brown himself was an immensely talented individual who ran a large, successful and complex business. He generally worked on a vast scale, establishing extensive plantations, changing landforms and creating lakes. Many examples of his landscapes survive and are open to the public, including Croome in Worcestershire, Petworth in West Sussex and Chatsworth in Derbyshire. At Blenheim he drowned the formal arrangement of water features, and the lower sections of Vanbrugh's great bridge that spanned them, beneath a particularly vast and impressive lake. By the time of his death in 1783 he had undertaken more than 250 commissions, mainly for the richest and most powerful figures in England. But by now there were several thousand landscape parks in the country. Some were designed by landowners and their head gardeners but many by professionals, including men like Nathaniel Richmond, William Emes or Richard Woods, who worked across much of England. Often dismissed as Brown's 'imitators', each brought his own twist to the new style, in ways that modern scholars have only recently begun to understand.

And there were other ways in which Brown was not the only show in town. Some people found the stripped-down,

LEFT The Leasowes, Shropshire, was developed by poet William Shenstone between 1743 and 1769.

OPPOSITE In 1763, the 4th Duke of Marlborough commissioned Lancelot 'Capability' Brown to redesign the parkland and gardens at Blenheim Palace, Oxfordshire.

almost minimalist simplicity of his manicured parklands boring, and at a number of places, including Painshill in Surrey, Stourhead and Kew south-west of London, more cluttered and evocative gardens, begun in the 1740s and '50s, continued to develop into the 1760s and '70s, and to attract hordes of appreciative visitors. Still older, geometric styles of gardening sometimes persisted in the manor house grounds of provincial squires, and even major landowners sometimes retained cherished geometric gardens. At Wrest Park in Bedfordshire the centrepiece of the garden remained the linear vista and canal, flanked by formal wildernesses, focused on Thomas Archer's magnificent pavilion, completed in 1711. Brown's activities were restricted to the peripheries of the gardens.

For there never was, in reality, a simple linear development in 18th-century garden design; and while there were certainly long-term continuities of development, these are not all best understood in terms of a single-minded quest for more 'natural' landscapes. One trend, continuing through the century, was the growing importance of the park, rather than the garden, as the principal setting for the mansion: no longer placed beside but increasingly wrapped around it, like an insulating blanket, and with Brown's perimeter belts ultimately obscuring close views of the working countryside. Another gradual, continuous development was the marginalization of useful, productive facilities from the landscapes of fashion, with orchards, fish ponds and kitchen gardens increasingly hidden from view, or placed at a distance from the house, something that again culminated in the works of Brown. These developments arguably reflected subtle shifts in the attitudes and lifestyles of the wealthy – a growing separation from the local community, an increasing withdrawal from active, direct involvement in useful production – which characterized this age of 'politeness'. But there are other connections we might make, other ways we might 'read' changing styles of garden and landscape design. Both Kent and Brown worked in some capacity as architects, and the building or modification of country houses, and the laying out of their grounds, usually went hand in hand. It is easy to see connections between, for example, the rise of Palladian architecture and the popularity of Kent's Italianate gardens; or between the crisp, elegant lines of the neo-classical house and the minimalist simplicity of Brown's parklands.

There is much we still have to learn about this fascinating period of garden history. But to appreciate the character and meaning of 18th-century gardens and parks we need, above all, to experience their surviving remains, albeit now often over-mature, significantly altered and with numerous later additions. And this is what we invite you to do, inspired by the essays on particular, iconic gardens of the period that occupy the pages to follow.

Tom Williamson

Castle Howard

North Yorkshire

–

**Nicholas Hawksmoor;
Sir John Vanbrugh;
Charles Howard, 3rd
Earl of Carlisle**

–

c. 1701-1730s

–

Registered Grade I

'Nobody had informed me that at one view I should see a palace, a town, a fortified city, temples on high places, woods worthy of being each a metropolis of the Druids, the noblest lawns in the world fenced by half the horizon, and a mausoleum that would tempt one to be buried alive ....'

Horace Walpole, 1772.

The old castle at Henderskelfe was inherited by Charles Howard, 3rd Earl of Carlisle, in 1692. In 1693 it was gutted by fire, and some ten years later he decided to build again on the same site. He commissioned William Talman to make designs, with George London providing a large formal setting of avenues and lakes. Talman fell out with his patron, who then turned to John Vanbrugh. Neither Carlisle nor Vanbrugh had any experience in building or landscaping although they had grand ideas. Carlisle was strongly influenced by a visit to Italy in 1690 and his familiarity with the classics. They sought the help of Nicholas Hawksmoor – who was experienced in practical matters – to realize Carlisle's vision of a classically inspired house and gardens to celebrate the family and its achievements. Vanbrugh died in 1726, Hawksmoor in 1736 and Carlisle in 1738. Together they worked to bring the extraordinary design to completion. London's regularly shaped lake and straight avenues were abandoned in favour of a varied and dramatic landscape with wide views.

The main approach from the south lies along a straight road rising and falling through fortified walls and gateways to an obelisk. A 'noble lawn' was made on the south of the house

OPPOSITE The garden façade of Castle Howard, the south terrace and the path to Wray Wood.

to Vanbrugh's innovative design, 'planted' with obelisks, vases and a central column – all soon swept away. In 1853, William Andrews Nesfield designed an elaborate parterre (replaced by the present grass and yew hedges) and the Atlas Fountain, so familiar from the film *Brideshead Revisited*.

Near the house and among the ancient trees of Wray Wood, a landscape inspired by classical mythology was created, with bastioned outer walls, winding walks, rocky caves, a stream and numerous statues, including a huge Apollo on a rocky plinth. By 1800 most of this had gone, but visitors' accounts and sketches and drawings by Hawksmoor, help to bring it back to life. It was clear-felled in the 1940s and replanted by James Russell in the 1970s. In the old kitchen garden, Russell made a Venus Garden using one of the Wray Wood statues, and the great Apollo on his plinth now stands nearby.

The old village street of Henderskelfe forms a curving path bordered with classical statuary from the house to Vanbrugh's four-porticoed Temple on the edge of the wood. From there, the visitor can see the New River and bridge, with the Mausoleum beyond, designed by Hawksmoor for Carlisle and his descendants. Further away is a giant pyramid containing a memorial to Lord William Howard, Carlisle's Elizabethan ancestor.

Despite changes made since, the main lines of the landscape survive, with most of the buildings. So, like Walpole, visitors today can marvel at the variety and novelty of this memorable landscape.

Sally Jeffery

Wrest Park

The gardens at Wrest Park were already established by the 17th century. In 1639, the poet and courtier Thomas Carew, delighted by a visit to Wrest, penned an ode to his hosts the 8th Earl of Kent (1583–1639) and his wife Elizabeth, celebrating both their generous hospitality and their watery landscape. He described Wrest as, 'This island Mansion, which, i'th' centre plac'd / Is with a double Crystall heaven embrac'd / In which our watery constellations floate / Our Fishes, Swans, our Water-man and Boat, …'.

By the early 18th century, that landscape had been fashionably marshalled into a series of canals, formal ponds, long avenues and walled gardens, in the Anglo-Dutch garden fashion of the late 17th century. Statues of both William III and his alter egos, Atlas and Neptune, graced the gardens, testifying to the political sympathies and astute political gardening of Anthony, 11th Earl of Kent (1645–1702) and his son Henry.

It was Henry (1671–1740) created 1st Duke of Kent, by Queen Anne, who ornamented the gardens with the distinctive Archer Pavilion named after its designer, Thomas Archer (once matched by a viewing 'house' on Cain Hill); a Bowling Green Pavilion and Stove House by the wonderfully named designer Batty Langley; as well as contributions by Giacomo Leoni and an obelisk to designs by William Kent.

Over a period of almost 40 years, the well-travelled Henry spent his own fortune and that of his two wives, on expanding his park and the woodland Great Garden, making walks and avenues, erecting obelisks and columns

Silsoe, Bedfordshire
-
Henry Grey,
1st Duke of Kent
-
1702 onwards
-
Registered Grade I

BELOW One of Earl de Grey's 1839 parterres restored by English Heritage.

OPPOSITE Chinese Pavilion commissioned by Jemima, Marchioness Grey and Philip Yorke, and set next to the Chinese Bridge.

and endlessly filling in old canals and creating new ones. Memorials brought a melancholy air to the grounds, as Henry's first wife and all his male heirs predeceased him, commemorated in the Duke and Duchess's Squares.

In 1740, the house and magnificent gardens, a repository of ancestral contributions, passed to Henry's granddaughter, Jemima, newly created Marchioness Grey (1723-97). Alongside her husband Philip Yorke, Jemima established Wrest as the centre of a coterie whose rural intellectualism embraced hermitages, cold baths, a root house and a flint knapped Mithraic Altar, which was said to have baffled eminent Cambridge antiquarians. Jemima's

letters to her female friends depict a rural Elysium, with honeysuckle, rambling roses and 'syringoes' (*Philadelphus coronarius*) scenting the woodland walks. In 1758-60, Lancelot 'Capability' Brown contributed 'professional assistance' softening the encircling waters, but Jemima did not permit alteration to her grandfather's formal layout of the woodland walks and avenues.

In 1839 Thomas Robinson, Earl de Grey (1781-1859), amateur architect and designer, swept away the old house (too close to the canals he declared) and created a magnificent French château 200 metres (650 feet) to the north, filing the new space with formal parterres to the

earl's own design. A 2.4-hectare (6-acre) walled kitchen garden provided luxuries for the family and employment for gardeners until the eventual sale of the estate in 1918.

Restored by English Heritage from 2010 onwards, the iconic view from the house terrace, across the formal parterres, down the Long Canal towards the distant Archer Pavilion is an unforgettable vista of garden fashion from the 17th to the 20th century, still 'embrac'd' in its 'double Crystall heaven'.

Twigs Way

ABOVE The view down the Long Canal to the Archer Pavilion, guarded by Neptune.

OPPOSITE A detail of the 1719 Map of 'Rest' Park by Edward Lawrence.

Studley Royal

Subjectively, the Aislabies' Studley Royal makes such extraordinary use of the topography in which it is set, that visitors over centuries have justly described it as 'the wonder of the North' (1732) and a 'masterpiece of human creative genius' (UNESCO, 1986). Objectively, as we now see after careful study, its progressive enlargement allowed experiment with (and preservation of) every key Georgian landscaping fashion. This palimpsest is all the more notable and successful for its remarkably early embrace of the values of 'nature' alongside 'art'.

Studley Royal as visited today consists of the most 'artful' part of the designed landscape, sometimes referred to as the Water Gardens, started in earnest around 1718. Crisp, geometric ponds, canals and more informal lakes, convey the River Skell through a dramatic, glacially formed valley rising to each side. The slopes were traversed by a web of interlocking paths (only a fraction of which remain accessible today) offering a diverse range of prospects of the water bodies and elegant garden buildings or statuary placed beside them. The journey through the gardens initially took one to a prospect of Fountains Abbey; the ruins themselves were drawn into the garden itself in 1767 as part of a 1.6-kilometre (1-mile) expansion up the Skell.

These glories obscure much else of the Aislabies' considerably greater vision. North of the water gardens lie the 134-hectare (330-acre) park, where the family home once stood. Too easily overlooked, the park was the crucial hub around which all the other components of the designed landscape linked, the origin point and destination

Ripon, North Yorkshire

-

The Aislabie family

-

1670–1781

-

Registered Grade I World Heritage Site

RIGHT The lead statue
of Bacchus in front of the
Temple of Piety.

of myriad circuit walks and rides. These included a route
south along the rugged Seven Bridges Valley (which would
be decorated with both classical-inspired structures, in the
style of Claude Lorrain and Chinese-style ones) to How
Hill, Studley's outlying prospect tower commanding the
whole estate and outwards for many miles. Lands between
Studley and Ripon were a considered 'estate landscape'
presaging arrival at the park's gates. From the 1740s more
substantial projects spread northwards to connect Studley
with two more gardens at Laver Banks and Hackfall (some
11 kilometres/7 miles distant). With extension embracing
the abbey these created overall circuits of 48 kilometres
(30 miles) or more, with journeys between highlights being
almost as significant as the highlights themselves. Sadly,
much of this creativity did not survive other pressures on
land use in the 19th century.

Father and son, John (1670–1742) and William Aislabie
(c. 1699–1781), seem in large part to have been their own
landscape gardeners. John knew John James, certainly
employed Colen Campbell, and most significantly consulted
Sir John Vanbrugh. William Aislabie was related by marriage
to Lord Burlington, and some of Kent's ideas seem to have
informed Studley. Fortunately for us today, William Aislabie's
heirs and successors (as his will instructed) diligently
conserved the core of his grounds, even if the extremities
withered. The loss of Studley Hall to fire in 1946 was perhaps
the most distracting moment in its history, creating today's
erroneous impression of 'a garden without a house'.

Mark Newman

Rousham Gardens

Rousham,
Oxfordshire
–
Charles Bridgeman
and William Kent
–
1721 onwards
–
Registered Grade I

OPPOSITE One of the great stone urns at the end of the Seven Arched Praeneste and Cow Castle.

BELOW William Kent's 'gothicized' mill with distant eye-catcher on the hill behind.

This remarkable garden represents the essence of William Kent's work. He is often hailed as the pioneer of the landscape garden: this suggests a natural look, but, although Horace Walpole considered him Dame Nature's first husband (the second was 'Capability' Brown), all his gardens contain geometry and regularity to some degree. At Rousham, as elsewhere, he worked on the foundation of an existing formal layout by Charles Bridgeman.

Bridgeman created a garden stretching from the house down to the River Cherwell. He worked for Colonel Robert Dormer from 1721. Robert died in 1737 and was succeeded by his brother, General James Dormer. James employed Kent to convert Bridgeman's layout into a perfect circuit garden containing surprises, illusion, variety and a series of pictures or tableaux, with buildings and sculpture carefully located for maximum impact in their setting. The result was described by Dmitry Shvidkovsky, a Russian visitor in the 1990s, as 'the springtime of the landscape garden'. It is also a very theatrical garden.

The historical circuit, which needs to be followed for full effect, is a subtle balance of 'hide and reveal'. Surprises include a Gothic Seat which becomes a cowshed seen from the other side and the view of Venus's Vale from below after emerging from the Lime Walk. The Praeneste arcade at the top of the Vale is invisible from the upper path that conceals the fact that one is walking over it.

The upper level contains sculpture in stone (*Lion Attacking a Horse, Dying Gaul*) in keeping with the military career of the General. Statues below are mostly of lead

and express the world of love and the countryside. Terms (figures on pillars) of Hercules and Pan above the Praeneste indicate the transition. The entrance and exit to the circuit are marked by terms of Minerva, the goddess of battle (entrance) and of wisdom (exit).

The lower level is characterized by a series of triangular formations. The first is the Palladian gate with figures of Flora and Plenty and the pediment above; Venus in her Vale had two Cupids on swans – the lines extend to Pan and Faunus; the Pyramid stands at the apex of a downward sloping lawn bordered by trees; and Bridgeman's vestigial amphitheatre contains Ceres, representing food, Bacchus, representing wine, and Mercury. In the house is a painting illustrating the Roman tag, 'Without Ceres and Bacchus, Venus [love] grows cold'.

Pan and Faunus stand as if on a stage, looking out over the Oxford countryside to the mill 'gothicized' by Kent and the eyecatcher arch on a distant hillside. The whole of Venus's Vale, a set piece with its twin cascades, evokes the garden at Villa Aldobrandini, Frascati, near Rome, probably seen by Kent during his long stay in Italy.

Walpole considered Rousham 'the most engaging of all Kent's works', and reckoned it was the perfect place for a philosophic retirement worthy of a Roman emperor.

Michael Symes

ABOVE *Lion Attacking a Horse*, a sculpture by Peter Scheemakers, 1740.

OPPOSITE The Long Border at Rousham.

St Paul's Walden Bury

The jewel that is the focus at St Paul's Walden Bury is an 18th-century wilderness. Laid out to accompany a new country home, it has survived remarkably intact under the stewardship of one family. A level piece of ground could have been selected for this mostly native woodland plantation; instead it dips and rises over the north Chilterns to great effect. A broad grass goosefoot path system slices long views from the house through the wood, with narrower paths and views cutting across. Each section of wood is bounded with high clipped hedging, originally hornbeam, now beech. Hedges, at one time used to manage livestock, here control the wildwood. It is a clever visual device. At the end of each ride there is an eye-catcher – a sculpture, building or the church that lies outside the estate – all to encourage you further.

Within the wood, meandering paths lead you to pools, urns or where the peonies self-seed. There is an extraordinary tranquillity here, perhaps from all the green, or the sunlight that falls between the trees, or because the ground is rich and deep in leaf mould. Spanning either side of one of the narrower grass paths is a large, hedged enclosure. It has a rotunda at the highest point, sphinxes, broad sculpted grass steps, a formal pond and another sculpture named the Running Footman by the family. In spring this area is full of orchids and primroses; in late August it was a soft blue haze of knapweed and scabious. Stephen Poliakoff's film, *Perfect Strangers*, revisits this enclosure to reveal the story behind an intriguing photograph taken here, echoing secret meetings in the

St Paul's Walden, Hertfordshire
–
Possibly Edward Gilbert; Mary Bowes, Mary Eleanor Bowes Lyon; Sir David and Sir Simon Bowes Lyon with Geoffrey Jellicoe (1936–90)
–
c. 1725–62; 1936–90
–
Registered Grade I

RIGHT Naturalizing spotted orchids may not have been envisaged by Geoffrey Jellicoe when he restored the Running Footman garden, but the effect is sublime.

OPPOSITE The Garden
Temple designed by
William Chambers for
a lake at Danson Park,
Kent, was rescued in 1961,
restored and relocated as
a focal point on the lake
at St Paul's Walden.

RIGHT Standing square
on to the central grass
allée, Hercules looks
sideways to the Organ
House. This scene is
almost 300 years old.

BELOW RIGHT The
wide central *allée* is a
visual lure to take a stroll,
but just who or what
might be hiding in the
mysterious wildwood
behind those hedges?

family's own history; it was through his eyes that I first
encountered St Paul's Walden Bury.

In 1936, Geoffrey Jellicoe was invited by Sir David
Bowes Lyon to help rescue the wilderness from its
deteriorating state. For Sir David and his sister Elizabeth,
then Duchess of York, this was their childhood home.
Both were serious gardeners and work on Royal Lodge at
Windsor Park was also commissioned from Jellicoe in 1936.

Jellicoe's involvement here is invisible mending,
replacing hedges, avenues, reconnecting views, encouraging
the search for appropriate replacement structures and
repairing the existing; he designed a delightful sequence
of steps to the Running Footman garden and restored
this area throughout. Jellicoe's connection with St Paul's
Walden Bury endured until the early 1990s, working with
two generations of Bowes Lyons, helping to breathe life
gently back into the wilderness. His last contribution was
an enclosed garden, a gift for Lady Bowes Lyon, on the west
side of the house. His first design was found not to fit as,
at 90, his measured pace had changed somewhat, but his
second design was implemented. There are copies of both
designs in the Landscape Institute archive at the Museum
of English Rural Life, part of a substantial collection of his
work. Another version of this design was deposited with the
Royal Academy when he was elected a Royal Academician
in 1991.

Annabel Downs

Gibside

OPPOSITE View down the Long Walk or Avenue of oak trees from the Chapel at Gibside.

BELOW The ruins of the Orangery that was added in 1772–74 by Mary Eleanor Bowes.

Gateshead, Tyne and Wear

–

Inspired by Stephen Switzer; executed by William Joyce

–

1731

–

Registered Grade I

The Gibside landscape is a remarkable survival of an extensive early 18th-century design, developed during the ownership of coal baron George Bowes (1721–60). Stephen Switzer drew up a plan in 1731 and supplied a further plan and trees for the grounds in 1732. The plans have not survived so we do not know how much they influenced the design. There is evidence that William Joyce, who was head gardener from 1732–36, was a key figure in executing the layout with the estate workforce. An estate map of 1767 by James Stephenson shows the executed layout.

A contour entrance drive provides a processional route through the estate to the pre-existing house at its focus. Axial vistas through the pleasure-ground woodland led the eye to contemporary architectural or other features; the three-roomed Bath House, for example, was accessed by a series of walks taking advantage of the natural landscape of the Derwent valley. The impressive 43-metre (141-foot) column to Liberty, intended as a statement of George Bowes's political allegiance to the Whigs, still dominates this part of the valley. The gothick banqueting house and Palladian stable block were the work of Daniel Garrett. The estate chapel which terminates the Long Walk/Avenue was designed by James Paine, with work starting in 1760. The Orangery was a subsequent addition (1772–74) by his daughter, Mary Eleanor Bowes, a keen botanist.

In the early 19th century, the old Jacobean hall was remodelled by Alexander Gilkie for John Bowes, 10th Earl of Strathmore, who also recovered the landscape from a period of decline. In the 1830s, a 30-metre (100-foot)

LEFT View from the Old Basin looking up the overgrown vista to the Column to Liberty, carved *in situ* by Christopher Richardson in 1756–57.

OPPOSITE Herbs and beds in the Walled Garden.

curvilinear vinery range was added to the walled garden and an orchid house followed. In mid-century, the orangery was reconstructed as a conservatory with a ridge-and-furrow glazed roof. Ornamental planting reflects the interests of later members of the Bowes Lyon family, notably John Bowes (founder of the Bowes Museum at Barnard Castle) and William Hutt (later Sir William, MP). In the 20th century, the late Queen Mother was an occasional visitor, and when he was Prince of Wales, King Charles III viewed the restoration of the garden.

The landscape fell into decline in the 20th century, with the plantings being felled in the 1930s, and post-war restocking of the woodland by Forestry Commission conifer plantations. The hall and other buildings became ruinous, but the quality and survival of the landscape was increasingly recognized from the 1950s, and it has undergone a gradual restoration since the 1960s, increasing in pace since the National Trust began to care for the core of the old estate from the 1990s onwards.

The combination of an enlightened local authority, national designation for both built and natural heritage and teamwork by conservation bodies, matched by successful fundraising, has resulted in a remarkable restoration. Although now a ruined shell, the hall remains as a focus for the landscape. The original layout and the wooded valley and parkland, which still has the feel of relatively undeveloped countryside close to Tyneside, makes the site a popular 'green lung' for the district.

Harry Beamish

West Wycombe

If ever a garden was imbued with the personality of its larger-than-life owner, it is West Wycombe. Every feature is coloured by Dashwood's interests and inclinations, and clouds of exaggeration and myth surround this extraordinary landscape of associations, some provocative. For 35 years Sir Francis Dashwood (1708–81) was the driving force of the Society of Dilettanti, famed in equal measure for excessive drinking and for serious study and support of archaeological expeditions to Greece and the Middle East.

The National Trust cares only for the 16-hectare (40-acre) pleasure ground adjoining the house, which overlooks the lake, created by damming the River Wye. Several Greek Revival buildings by Nicholas Revett from c. 1770 include the west portico of the house, known as the Temple of Bacchus, which is mirrored on the eastern side; both look like independent garden buildings. Most notorious of the features is the Temple of Venus (c. 1748) on a mound - originally surrounded by 25 lead sculptures - and Venus's Parlour at the foot of the mound, an unmistakable representation of a vagina, with architectural wings (legs) on each side.

There is also much of historic interest in the eastern park and in the hill that dominates the gardens, with its Hellfire Caves, the Mausoleum and the church on the top surmounted by a golden ball, visible for miles around: it held up to a dozen people and was reckoned by a visitor 'the best Globe tavern I was ever in.'

It is a garden of pairs, one feature echoing another, such as the shoemaker's cottage, St Crispin's, built as a petite church with tower (and later a spire) as if to mock the

West Wycombe,
Buckinghamshire
-
Sir Francis
Dashwood,
2nd Baronet
(Lord Le Despencer
from 1763)
-
1735–81
-
Registered Grade I

RIGHT Nicholas Revett's Music Temple, 1778–82, on its island, with the church on the hill in the background.

OPPOSITE ABOVE AND BELOW 'Rococo' cascade, lake and church on top of the 'Hell-Fire' hill, and Lake, 'Walton Bridge' and Temple of Venus engraved by William Woollett after William Hannan, 1757.

RIGHT Temple of Venus with 'Venus's Parlour' below.

BELOW RIGHT Lead copy, probably by John Cheere, of the *Apollo Belvedere* in the Temple of Apollo.

genuine church on the hill. Yet Dashwood was also jointly responsible for abridging *The Book of Common Prayer* to shorten services for the cold and elderly during the winter. There is a unifying theme of local flintwork as dressing for many of the garden buildings, and a pyramid finial is regularly used.

Liberty is an important theme in the gardens, as it was at Stowe (a likely source of inspiration). Though politically an independent, Dashwood was brought into Whig Opposition circles, for which liberty was a watchword. An inscription over the arch of the Temple of Apollo reads 'Sacred to liberty and friendship'. This is appropriated from Stowe, but is somewhat mischievous as the temple was used for cock-fighting and as a lavatory.

Although Dashwood's was the guiding hand, surveyors, architects and in one case a pupil of 'Capability' Brown, Thomas Cook, assisted in constructing and executing the work. Later in the century, post-Dashwood, Humphry Repton was brought in to tidy up what had become overgrown and too dark and shady. He thinned out trees and also removed what he regarded as meaningless architectural touches.

There was much interest from America and the continent. Benjamin Franklin was a regular visitor, and Prince Franz of Anhalt-Dessau was much impressed, especially by the bridges. In the Green Frog dinner service made for Catherine the Great by Wedgwood, 15 pieces represented views of West Wycombe.

Michael Symes

Painshill

Cobham, Surrey

–

The Hon. Charles Hamilton

–

1738–73

–

Registered Grade I

The appeal of Painshill is based on its combination of nature and views. It was 'designed nature', working from an unpromising stretch of land that was substantially 'dreary heath' as described at the time, but the result looked natural. The art consisted in focusing the views, which were mostly internal, so that features came in and out of sight and were viewed from different angles and distances. Painshill unites skilful and subtle design, including illusion and surprise, employing the techniques of an artist (grouping, perspective, light and shade, open and closed), with Hamilton's great love of planting, especially recent introductions of trees from abroad, creating what is, in effect, an arboretum.

The lake is central to the layout, and has always created illusion, both in its deceptive size and in its appearance – lake, river, creek, even the semblance of a canal, in turn. The circuit embodies Hamilton's application of a tenet of 18th-century design, namely that the foot should never travel to a distant object (usually a building) the same way the eye has travelled, after seeing it initially from afar. The arc of distant buildings, all in different architectural styles, seen near the start of the circuit at the Gothic Temple, beckons the visitor to see them more closely. The Temple of Bacchus, recently reinstated, is the architectural showpiece, and is reached late in the circuit as a climax. The 'crystal grotto', on its island dotted with imported marine rock, is outstanding in its elaboration and impact. The currently operational vineyard was originally reckoned to be the leading example in the land.

LEFT Painshill Park as seen from the Turkish Tent at the end of the circuit.

The layout is still intact, with restoration as close as possible to how Hamilton left it in 1773. Some of his trees remain, and there are few signs of alterations. Among celebrity visitors of the time were Benjamin Franklin; the Abbé Nolin, royal nurseryman to Louis XV and Louis XVI, who supplied Hamilton with seeds and plants from the French colonies; Prince Franz of Anhalt-Dessau, who was inspired by his English tours to create the Gartenreich at Dessau-Wörlitz; Princess Dashkova from Russia; a party of leading international botanists; and Horace Walpole, the ultimate 'arbiter of taste', who pronounced the western wood an exemplar of forest or savage gardening.

The process of creating the garden involved laying out the landscape first, including softening and reducing a previous large formal plot in hippodrome shape on top of the vineyard hill. Plantings were part of the first phase, with some cedars dating from the mid-1740s, and the lake and vineyard were developed. The earliest buildings were a short-lived Chinese seat (c. 1748) and the Hermitage by 1752, but the spate of garden architecture had to wait until the late 1750s. Distinction was drawn between the 'garden', a large, broad crescent with ancient and new ornamental planting, and the 'park', a plainer, open area that could be used as pasture.

Since 1981 the Painshill Park Trust has been restoring and maintaining a site that had become derelict and overgrown. In 1998 it won the Europa Nostra prize for exemplary restoration.

Michael Symes

Painswick Rococo Garden

Painswick is the country's sole surviving complete rococo garden. In 1738, wealthy landowner Benjamin Hyett, began to lay out the small combe or valley behind his house as a fanciful pleasure garden for entertaining. Serpentine paths along the sides of the valley form a circuit walk through woodland, dotted with follies of different architectural styles. There was a grand formal vegetable garden and springs fed a cold bath and pond.

Near the entrance a gothic summerhouse, the Eagle House (Grade II*), provides views across the valley to the Doric seat and, originally, to a pedimented arch. Further on through woodland stood the Red House (Grade II*), an elaborate garden pavilion with ogee-headed openings and a fireplace inside. From there the path led west to the Exedra, a white-painted wooden screen with gothic arches, surmounted with battlements and pinnacles. In front of the Exedra was a small formal garden with a pool, and a kitchen garden of wedge-shaped beds around a small circular dipping pond.

The garden was painted by Thomas Robins in 1748, and the landscape and many of its buildings may have been designed by him, though there is no proof. When fashions changed the garden became neglected. The estate was much enlarged in the first half of the 19th century by William Henry Hyett, an MP and agricultural scientist, and in 1847 he acquired the freehold, which passed to his son and, through his heiresses, to Lord Dickinson in 1955.

In 1984, historians Timothy Mowl and Roger White saw Robins' painting in an exhibition and wrote an article

Stroud, Gloucestershire
–
Possibly Thomas Robins
–
1738–48
–
Registered Grade II*

OPPOSITE The Exedra with its backdrop of ancient beech trees, seen from the dipping pond in the Kitchen Garden.

about the garden for the Garden Trust's journal *Garden History*. This inspired Lord and Lady Dickinson to restore it. The garden had survived relatively well until the mid-20th century when it was planted with conifers. Despite being neglected and overgrown, it was therefore possible to clear the timber and restore the garden.

The initial restoration was based on the 1748 painting and focused on reintroducing many of the features that had been lost. These included the Eagle House pavilion, the Exedra and the Kitchen Garden with its natural pools. Buildings that survived, such as the Red House and the Eagle House arch were conserved. The garden is maintained with planting and landscaping that is as close as practicable to the spirit of the rococo era and is recognizably that of Robins' painting. In 1998, a maze designed by Professor Angela Newling was laid out to the west of the Exedra, to mark the 250th anniversary of the painting.

The garden is now cared for by the charitable Painswick Rococo Garden Trust. It is maintained by four permanent gardeners, and a team of over 40 volunteers, working to a conservation plan. Recent conservation projects include reinstating a small vineyard on the slope above the Kitchen Garden, following the Robins painting. Many visitors come early in the year to enjoy the carpet of over five million snowdrops (*Galanthus* spp.), which includes some rare varieties, as well as in the summer to experience this unique rococo pleasure garden.

Marion Mako

Alnwick Castle

Scholars will argue over the origins of Romanticism. Some point to Jean-Jacques Rousseau, others to Johann Herder and Goethe, but they all agree, with a nod to Coleridge and Wordsworth and the value that they placed on individual experience, that Romanticism came late to England. A visit to Alnwick Castle however might caution the scholars that an unquestioned reliance on the written word makes for glib history.

There is enough to enjoy in the immediate environs of the castle, where from 1996 the 12th Duchess of Northumberland has forged new gardens with echoes of Renaissance Europe and has woven around them her celebrated tree house and Lilidorei, the elf village. There is plenty too by way of distraction in the North Demesne, opposite the castle on the far side of the River Aln. The landscaping there had been begun by the duke's forester, Thomas Call, from the early 1760s, but 'Capability' Brown and his men took over in 1769, and they were responsible for its clumps and paddocks and the weirs in the river, making of the Aln another Derwent, as it flows through the park at Chatsworth.

Wonderful though both these are, they are trumped, for history and unmatched authenticity, by Hulne Park. Straddling the river on the west side of the castle, this park has been walled for 700 years, and to see Hulne today is to imagine that these walls were made not to confine deer, but to protect intact the 400 hectares (1,000 acres) of medieval England that they contain. In 1751, 19 years before Wordsworth was born, Hugh Percy, the 1st Duke of Northumberland (1714–86) and his wife Elizabeth (1716–76),

**Alnwick,
Northumberland**
–
Thomas Call
–
1751
–
Registered Grade I

OPPOSITE This aerial photograph shows the scale of Hulne Park.

BELOW The Grand Cascade at Alnwick, inspired by the Renaissance gardens at the Villa Lante in Italy.

OPPOSITE Brizlee Tower was built in 1781 for the Duke of Northumberland in remembrance of his wife, Lady Elizabeth Seymour, who died in 1776.

RIGHT A statue of a monk stands beside entrance to the Nine Year Hole. The Hole and Tower share that parentage of imagination without limits.

with the help of Thomas Call, set to work here. They began with a plantation on the sides of Brizlee Hill, to which the Duchess would add winding walks and a crude cave, the Nine Year Hole, said to be the haunt of robbers, calling it Carmel (God's orchard). In 1755, they moved on to Hulne Priory, the extensive ruins of which lay within the site, and the Duchess made that too a gothick pleasure ground. By 1765, with the help of Robert Adam, they had designed the tower on Brizlee Hill, completed in 1781 after the Duchess's death; too tall, with too many windows – not quite gothick, not Moorish, but entirely fantastical, here her imagination gave the final stamp to the park.

Its walks along the river, solitary and dark; its wild cliffs; the dizzying number of drives and bridges across the river; the hands-on involvement of the Duke and Duchess, freely acknowledged; their references to other civilizations and

to the deep past of England – all engage the imagination, all impact upon the sensibilities of the individual – all are reflected in the tower's inscription:

> 'Circumspice / Ego omnia ista sum Dimensus; / Mei sunt ordines, / Mea Descriptio: / Multae etiam istarum arborum / Mea manu sunt satae'
> ['Look around/I am the measurer of everything here/ The ranks [of trees] are mine/The design is mine/Many of these trees are even sown with my own hand']

This is a park that the Romantics would have recognized as their own. Go in at the Stocking Gate. Bring a picnic. Do not hurry. Entry is free.

John Phibbs

Royal Botanic Gardens, Kew

Kew Gardens have had a special significance within both garden and scientific history spanning 300 years. The footprint of today's gardens grew from the merging of the Richmond and Kew royal estates in the 18th century, with landscaping at Richmond Gardens undertaken by Charles Bridgeman from the 1720s, and garden buildings by William Kent. In 1759, the household accounts of Princess Augusta mention the cultivation of a physic garden (a botanical garden specifically for medicinal plants) on the site for the first time, and it is this which is taken to mark the foundations of a scientific garden. By 1768, when John Hill published a catalogue of plants growing at Kew, *Hortus Kewensis*, there were 2,700 species of plants grown; a year later, when the second edition was printed, this had increased to 3,400.

The development of the botanic garden is necessarily part of a wider history of the royal family. The estate has also been home to a number of royal residences including Kew Palace and Queen Charlotte's cottage, both now managed by Historic Royal Palaces. The gardens contain traces of this legacy as a courtly setting and notable features created by leading designers include the extant Great Pagoda, built by William Chambers in 1761 (which was once flanked by the now lost Alhambra and Mosque), the Hollow Walk, now known as the Rhododendron Dell, created in 1773 by 'Capability' Brown' and William Nesfield's 1840s Arboretum. One of the most striking features of the gardens today is Decimus Burton's glass Palm House of 1844–48 which exemplifies the combination of beauty with engineering ingenuity.

Kew, London
–
Among others,
Charles Bridgeman;
William Kent;
William Chambers;
'Capability' Brown;
William Nesfield;
Decimus Burton
–
1759
–
Registered Grade I
World Heritage Site

RIGHT The Temperate House, designed by Decimus Burton, opened in 1863.

ABOVE LEFT The Pagoda, built in 1861 by Sir William Chambers.

LEFT The Rhododendron Dell. Originally 'Capability' Brown's Hollow Walk, it was created in 1773 and planted with rhododendrons in 1850.

ABOVE Pancratium caribaeum *and a Passion Flower, Jamaica*, by plantswoman Marianne North, c. 1872.

OPPOSITE Decimus Burton's Palm House, built between 1844 and 1848, comprises 16,000 panes of glass.

The scientific story of Kew as a world-class botanic garden really begins with Sir Joseph Banks, a scientific polymath and explorer. While on Captain Cook's voyage to the South Seas, Banks sent seeds back to Kew and on his return to Britain became Kew's first unofficial director under King George III. From this point onwards, Kew became a central focus for plants, botanic knowledge and discovery within the growing British Empire. A succession of botanists followed Banks in the 19th century, including William and Joseph Hooker who led the development of economic botany through the collecting, cataloguing and utilization of natural resources from around the world. This connection with global botanic riches can also be seen in the paintings of Marianne North, who recorded plants in their locations as far afield as Jamaica, Brazil, India and Japan. These are still displayed in the gallery she funded and is named after her at Kew, which opened in 1882.

Kew has long been a resort for the plant-seeking public. Limited access to visitors had been granted from George III's reign, but from the 1820s public access was gradually widened, and it became a popular Victorian attraction. Today Kew, with its sister garden, Wakehurst, in Sussex, welcome over 2 million visitors a year. Kew is also home to over 68,000 living plants, as well as other collections such as the Millennium Seed Bank, a world-class herbarium of dried specimens and an economic botany collection.

Clare Hickman

Hafod

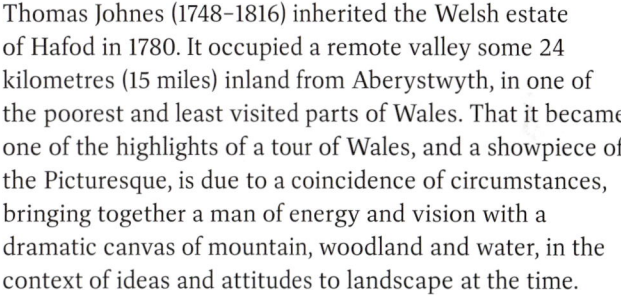

OPPOSITE The
rustic bridge on the
Gentleman's Walk.

BELOW Lady's Walk with
river, rock and roots.

Pont-rhyd-y-groes,
Ceredigion
–
Thomas Johnes
–
1780 onwards
–
Registered Grade I

Thomas Johnes (1748–1816) inherited the Welsh estate
of Hafod in 1780. It occupied a remote valley some 24
kilometres (15 miles) inland from Aberystwyth, in one of
the poorest and least visited parts of Wales. That it became
one of the highlights of a tour of Wales, and a showpiece of
the Picturesque, is due to a coincidence of circumstances,
bringing together a man of energy and vision with a
dramatic canvas of mountain, woodland and water, in the
context of ideas and attitudes to landscape at the time.

Johnes grew up at Croft Castle in North Herefordshire.
His near neighbours were Richard Payne Knight (also his
cousin) of Downton Castle and Sir Uvedale Price of Foxley.
Influenced by their ideas and with a liberal education behind
him, he set out to use his inherited wealth to realize his
dreams at Hafod. Here he would build a house in the Gothic
style, in the midst of a landscape that could be moulded to
his ideal design and provide space to pursue his interests. At
Hafod, innovation, art and learning would flourish. Visitors
would experience not only an overall impression of beauty
and grandeur but also enjoy access to a series of views:
pictures, composed by Nature with assistance from the hand
of Art, to delight the senses and inspire the poet or painter.

In making Hafod's existence and attractions known he
was greatly assisted by the publication of his friend George
Cumberland's book, *An Attempt to Describe Hafod*, published
in 1796. By this date Johnes was already established in
his new house with his wife, Jane, a keen gardener, and
his young daughter, Mariamné, who became a talented
naturalist. He had laid out his first two walks – described in

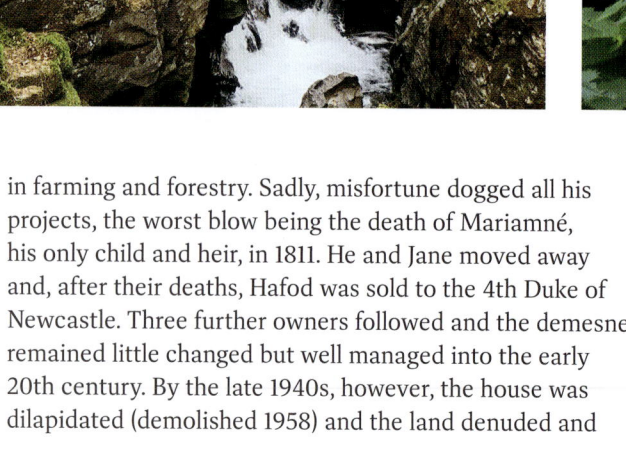

ABOVE Sketch of the Ystwyth gorge and chain bridge, by Laura Elizabeth Sanders, 1835.

RIGHT The same view today. The bridge was restored by the Hafod Trust in 2003.

OPPOSITE *Chelone obliqua* and Coade stone gateway in Mrs Johnes's Flower Garden.

detail by Cumberland – where the visitor was led through an unfolding picturesque drama of river scenery, rocks, cascades, ancient trees, rustic bridges and caves. To enable his visitors to explore Hafod at leisure, Johnes provided accommodation nearby, building a new inn, the Hafod Arms, 6 kilometres (4 miles) away at Devil's Bridge.

Johnes continued to create additional walks and make changes to his landscape, as well as pursuing his interests in farming and forestry. Sadly, misfortune dogged all his projects, the worst blow being the death of Mariamné, his only child and heir, in 1811. He and Jane moved away and, after their deaths, Hafod was sold to the 4th Duke of Newcastle. Three further owners followed and the demesne remained little changed but well managed into the early 20th century. By the late 1940s, however, the house was dilapidated (demolished 1958) and the land denuded and

scarred. In 1950 the estate was purchased for the Forestry Commission, and large areas were planted with softwoods.

The initiative to restore the historic landscape began in 1991, soon after the formation of the Welsh Historic Gardens Trust, and transferred to the Hafod Trust in 1994. Documentary research, archaeological surveys and landscape analysis enabled the restoration of the network of walks, necessitating the building of ten bridges of varying size and design. Views were recreated and areas of open ground, including Mrs Johnes's Flower Garden, restored.

In 2022, following a lease agreement with the landowners, the Welsh Government, responsibility for the historic landscape passed to the National Trust, who will continue the legacy of this internationally important site.

Jennie Macve

Tatton Park

One of the delights of Tatton Park in Cheshire is that new landscape features have been added and cherished over several centuries, giving it examples of many moments of garden history.

The garden heart of Tatton is a Victorian Italianate terrace, which sits below a neo-classical hall built by Samuel and Lewis Wyatt between 1780 and 1813. This formal garden offers paths and parterres around a square pool with Triton statue, before drawing us to a half-moon balustrade overlooking the parkland to one of the 'meres' for which Cheshire is known. The landscape park was designed in the 18th century – 'Capability' Brown and William Emes offered advice, but it was Humphry Repton at the end of the century whose proposals were actually implemented. The Tatton meres were to broaden Repton's experience of landscapes: 'it has often been asserted by authors of gardening, that all pieces of fresh water must come under one of these descriptions, – a lake, a pool, a river, or a rivulet: but since my acquaintance with Cheshire, I am inclined to add the meer, as an intermediate term between the lake and the pool; it being, frequently, too large to be deemed a pool, and too small, as well as too round in its form, to deserve the name of a lake.'

Some of Tatton's most captivating gardens are actually indoors. In 1818, Lewis Wyatt built a large sandstone conservatory, and a few decades later, in 1859, Joseph Paxton designed an atmospheric L-shaped red brick fernery, which survives today, filled with ferns and tree ferns from New Zealand and Australia, its entrance

Knutsford, Cheshire

–

Humphry Repton, Joseph Paxton and Lewis Wyatt

–

1782 onwards

–

Registered Grade II*

OPPOSITE An Italianate terrace and formal garden still provides a beautiful setting for the neo-classical hall.

BELOW The L-shaped fernery designed by Joseph Paxton in 1859.

something of a charming surprise behind an unassuming domestic-style door. In front of the conservatory is Charlotte's Garden, named for Lady Charlotte Egerton, which, although now somewhat understated, is an unusually surviving Regency flower garden.

A Broad Walk leads through ornamental trees and shrubs, past a maze of 1700 design, and the Golden Brook pool, and out towards the park. Its end is marked by a small copy of the Choragic Monument of Lysicrates in Athens, erected in the 1830s to commemorate Wilbraham Egerton's Grand Tour. A further international element was added in 1910 by the 3rd Baron Egerton, who brought in Japanese workmen to design and lay out a Japanese Garden, including stone lanterns, bridges, a thatched tea house and a Shinto shrine.

The nostalgic romance of the early 20th century also left its scent at Tatton, when a Rose Garden was laid out for Lady Anna Egerton, with steps from the working walled Kitchen Garden leading to an intimate, romantic courtyard filled with a pergola, statuary, sunken pool and tiny tea house. It connects to a later Tower Garden, in which yew hedges and brick walls form an enclosed garden around a crenelated, two-storey tower from the 18th century.

Today Tatton Park is run as a partnership between the National Trust and Cheshire East Council, after the last Lord Egerton, Maurice, died in 1958.

Linden Groves

OPPOSITE In 1910 the 3rd Baron Egerton brought a team of Japanese workmen to lay out Tatton's iconic Japanese Garden.

ABOVE Tatton's walled Kitchen Garden is still planted productively with fruit, vegetables and cutting flowers.

RIGHT A copy of the Choragic Monument of Lysicrates terminates the Broad Walk.

GARDENS IN THE 19ᵀᴴ CENTURY

Today's nation of gardeners originated in the 19th century when the middle classes acquired the space, time and inclination to garden. Space in the expanding suburbs, time freed up from working in the fields when life moved to the city, and the desire to take up the new hobby of gardening for the promise of 'a healthy mind in a healthy body' and a 'prim' garden. This legacy has one overriding obstacle: surviving 19th-century suburban gardens are very rare. They have succumbed to division, development, decay and the scattering of their families' archives. However, many of the trends they made their own are evident in surviving larger gardens. This was also an era of civic pride, reflected in the creation of public parks and cemeteries, and of lavish display in the country homes of newly wealthy landowners.

Humphry Repton participated in one of the earliest and most fundamental of 19th-century changes, the rise of the flower garden. When he launched his career in 1788, Repton emphasized continuity by pigeonholing himself as 'a follower' of 'Capability' Brown, evoking landscape parks, lakes and belts of trees. However, by his death in 1818 many of his commissions had been defined by flowers. At Ashridge in Hertfordshire his Red Book proposals of around 1811 included an oval 'Rosarium' to be set among a string of floral spaces (or 'episodes' as he described them elsewhere.) Recent research has suggested that the simultaneously flowering pink ground-cover roses, encircled by swags of yet more pink climbing roses, which he envisaged for Ashridge could not have been sourced by the nursery trade at the time. Other gardens dedicated to roses were emerging elsewhere. One of the earliest was laid out at Chiswick House, London, around 1804, and this trend was encouraged by at least one London nursery's printed list of around 300 different roses with diagrams for suggested layouts. Flower gardens in all their forms – not just those given over to roses – would go on to define the 19th century because they fitted well with middle-class aspirations to garden and crystalized many aspects of Victorian culture.

LEFT The Nuneham Courtenay rose garden. Edward Adveno Brooke, *The Gardens of England*, 1856.

OPPOSITE William Nesfield's parterre at Witley Court.

New technology, shifting politics and the expansion of Empire were all shrinking the globe and facilitating foreign plant introductions. Increasingly, commercially minded nurseries were taking advantage of cheap print, new prepaid postage stamps and expanding railway networks to market and distribute seeds and plants more efficiently. The urge to collect and classify the natural world was being studied through new local natural history societies running their own regular field trips, while the growing catalogue of garden plants was encouraging dedicated collections, especially of ferns and orchids, both among those with inherited wealth and those establishing new fortunes. Even architecture obliged with new bay windows, verandas, trellis-clad walls and conservatories, anchoring the flower garden to the parlour window, where it appeared as an extension to the home.

Before 1840 flowers were usually displayed in solitary beds or haphazard groupings of circular, oval or amoeba-shaped beds. Ringed with willow, hazel or timber (as suggested by Repton for Brighton's Royal Pavilion) such features were known as baskets, and some even sported 'handles' as frames for climbing plants. The domesticity of these features, with an edging imitating a picture frame, sat well in almost any suburban garden and they were used by the horticultural writer Robert Mangles around his home at Whitmore Lodge, near Sunninghill, Berkshire (by 1829) and by Louisa Lawrence at her home in Drayton Green, Ealing (by 1833); a well-publicized favourite of the writer John Claudius Loudon.

Around the same time, the abolition of the glass tax and advances in glass manufacture improved glasshouses, and made them increasingly affordable. Foreign exotics became an economic alternative to established hardy herbaceous and perennial plants. These tender plants lent themselves to temporary displays that could ameliorate the effect of urban pollution. Bedding, as it became known, morphed into a range of planting traditions between the 1830s and the 1870s using new plants and importantly, responding to the growing taste for bright colour in people's daily lives.

Before the 1850s, colour attracted little attention beyond the artist's studio until a synthetic dye,

rapidly nicknamed 'Perkin's purple' after its inventor, revolutionized ladies' fashion while Owen Jones's lavishly illustrated *Grammar of Ornament* analyzed the previously overlooked contribution of colour to architecture and the decorative arts. At the same time, regular new horticultural magazines led by Loudon's quarterly *Gardener's Magazine*, launched in the 1820s, provided gardeners with a platform for debate, and colour was a hot topic.

Initially, strongly contrasting pairings like the vibrant red 'Tom Thumb' geraniums and brilliant yellow calceolarias used by Joseph Paxton around the Crystal Palace after its move to Sydenham Park, were in favour. Paxton began his career working under his brother within the long-established system of on-the-job training that saw apprentices rise through the ranks to become under gardeners, journeymen, foremen and eventually head gardeners, by serving time in different departments (glasshouse, kitchen garden, fruit and pleasure garden), and sometimes moving from one estate to another. A little creative accounting regarding his age enabled Paxton to leave his brother for a place at the recently established Horticultural Society of London's training garden in Chiswick, which in turn propelled him to Chatsworth, where he developed such an extraordinary reputation for horticultural excellence that other young gardeners, in their turn, sought him out as a mentor. One of his most widely publicized achievements was to bring the first English example of the South American waterlily, *Victoria amazonica*, into flower at Chatsworth by housing it in a new hothouse of his own design. From this Paxton applied his structural understanding to the design of the iconic Crystal Palace and his undoubted commercial acumen to a range glasshouses widely marketed under the slogan 'hothouses for the millions'.

CANNA GÉANT.   RICINUS VARIABILIS SPLENDENS.   HELIANTHUS ARGOPHYLLUS STRIATIFLORUS FLORE PLENO

Planting taste eventually shifted away from the strident colour contrasts favoured by Paxton at the Crystal Palace towards colours adjacent, rather than opposite to one another, on the colour wheel. Many commentators and gardeners wanted to establish their individuality and debates developed around minor details such as the pros and cons of dot plants (a single plant of a contrasting colour or height usually at the centre of a bed) or the contribution of foliage and sky to a colour scheme. In 1854 a retired Head Gardener from Shrubland Hall in Suffolk, Donald Beaton, argued in the *Cottage Gardener* that the inescapable expanse of blue sky seen in every view from the terraces of the Crystal Palace, combined with the white of the gardens' fountains and the glass of the structure itself, was the reason behind the success of Paxton's contrasting reds and yellows.

At Shrubland Hall Beaton had previously championed a type of bedding popularly known as 'ribbon planting', in which long, narrow, parallel rows of flowering plants in a range of colours were inspired by his mistress's Berlin wool work, a popular Victorian handicraft. During the 1860s the increasing diversity of foliage plants such as cannas, solanums, *Ricinus* and *Dieffenbachia* (familiar today as a house plant) could be massed together to create another temporary display known as the subtropical garden. While new, low and slower-growing plants, typically *Alternanthera* and *Echeveria*,

ushered in carpet bedding in which Jane Loudon, wife of John and an early champion of garden publications for women, saw the domestic allusion of a Turkey carpet.

Bedding was enthusiastically adopted in some public parks (as well as private gardens) as it encapsulated one of the two key objectives that underpinned such new civic ventures. Exuberant public bedding could be read as a display of civic pride, while the establishment of a new park might embody the same aspirations for education and improvement exhibited in new public libraries, art galleries, museums and reading rooms. Free parks open to all began to appear from the 1840s, but wouldn't take off in any number until the 1870s, when local authorities had the necessary legal powers to raise funds and invest in such projects. Some, such as Paxton's Birkenhead Park, which opened in the 1840s, were driven by commerce as much as they were by aesthetics. They sculpted earth and water, aping a country estate for owners of new housing developed simultaneously around the perimeter. This model preferred traditional trees and shrubberies over new-fangled bedding. Another approach showcased the need for recreation to improve the health of the expanding urban population. This set the priorities for schemes such as Liverpool's Sefton Park in the 1860s, where Édouard André applied Parisian ideas that divided a site into interlocking ellipses and teardrop shapes dedicated to individual sports, screening one from the next by shrubberies. Even here, where sport dominated, space was set aside for floral displays.

Today the Royal Parks maintain the shape of the beds and the planting patterns specified in the original designs for the Avenue Walk in London's Regent's Park drawn up by William Nesfield in the 1860s. Beds such as these, laid out on flat ground to create a symmetrical pattern inspired by historic designs and known as parterres, became highly fashionable during the middle decades of the 19th century. Other examples by Nesfield included a lost parterre from the 1840s at Alton Towers in Staffordshire, recreating the curlicues and arabesques of 17th-century designs, particularly drawing on French designers. Another of his designs from the 1850s for Witley Court in Worcestershire incorporated hard materials, typically crushed brick or shell, with a range of coloured minerals to inject vital winter interest in any important view from a house.

Nesfield's interest in historic French designs also points to 19th-century eclecticism; an eagerness to borrow and mix styles from different sources and periods. Architecturally inspired examples leave the firmest garden traces running, as they do, from the earliest years of the century in the 'Hindoo' gardens at Sezincote, Gloucestershire, to the mid-century Pagoda Fountain at Alton Towers, and on through a rash of red lacquered bridges inspired by willow-pattern plates, of which the most familiar must be that at Biddulph Grange in Staffordshire.

A widening plant palette, growing number of tender species and rise in hobby gardening inevitably pushed the quest for horticultural knowledge and skill up the national agenda where it became entwined in another new, chameleon-like concept, the gardenesque. The term was introduced (without definition) by Loudon in a book review published in the *Gardener's Magazine* during the 1830s. From there it attached itself to an existing approach to planting in which individual specimens were showcased in the somewhat spotty, haphazard arrangements of small beds discussed above. As the century progressed, the gardenesque acquired a further layer of meaning as a middle way through discussions of style, where it stood somewhere between the

18th-century origins of the rough picturesque and the artful geometry of a Nesfield parterre. In this form the gardenesque became a mixed, middle or irregular style and was seen in villa gardens and in the pleasure grounds of larger estates. Treading this middle path in the work of designers such as Edward Kemp, the gardenesque came to symbolize a network of serpentine paths between specimen shrubs and trees, which framed an inner terrace and flower garden.

Just as Parisian design had influenced Sefton Park, so the cemetery of Père-Lachaise, opened on the edge of Paris in 1804, suggested the picturesque as an appropriate aesthetic for another new type of civic landscape: cemeteries. A collection of privately owned cemeteries of picturesque design in a ring around London (later nicknamed the Magnificent Seven) were established during the 1830s and 1840s to provide a middle-class alternative to the squalor of overcrowded urban graveyards. By the time local authorities accepted cemeteries as part of their brief, Loudon had published detailed guidance on their ideal location, layout, planting and maintenance regime. He championed chalky, gravelly soil (for the increased speed of decomposition); evergreen over deciduous planting (for the absence of decaying foliage and an innate sense of solemnity); and, an orderly grid-like pattern for the graves (for ease of access and maintenance). Loudon saw cemeteries as one of the few situations where flower beds were inappropriate, given the unfortunate associations of freshly dug earth.

Returning to the private garden, rusticity and rockeries also evolved as design themes. At the turn of the century, Repton had placed a rustic *cottage orné*, with a thatched and bark-covered timber exterior, at the edge of the Woburn Abbey pleasure grounds in Bedfordshire, which played well against a sophisticated, richly furnished and painted interior. From the 1860s such rough and artful interpretations of the rustic were recast by middle-class gardeners in search of economy. Archways were used to straddle garden paths that led to uncomfortable-looking benches and every variety of building from rotating summerhouses to reading rooms. James Shirley Hibberd, the preferred author of the amateur gardener, explored this trend exhaustively in middle-class homes in his *Rustic Adornments for Homes of Taste* (1856).

RIGHT Sundial in the garden of Stone Hall, Essex.

Eighteenth-century rockwork with similar origins to the rustic transitioned its way through the century thanks to popular fascination with geology (crystallized at Biddulph Grange), and an interest in new materials (in the deceptive rockwork created by the Pulham family at sites such as Highnam, Gloucestershire) before also reverting to an economic motif for the middle classes.

The bark of new conifers brought from North and South America during the 1830s and from the slopes of the Himalayas in the 1840s resonated with these early interests in the rough and the rustic. Mid-century pinetums (a subgroup of the arboretum) at Biddulph Grange and Bicton Park in Devon were planted as picturesque displays rather than scientific collections. William Barron, a professional gardener (and later a successful nurseryman and author) emphasized the careful combination of leaf forms, habit and colours in his mid-century evergreen plantings for Elvaston Castle in Derbyshire, while from the 1870s, the writer and plantsman William Robinson began a move against all forms of transient floral display. He dismissed the architectural terraces necessary to provide a raised outdoor viewing point from which to appreciate the patterns of bedding, dubbing them 'railway embankment' gardens. Robinson's influential book *The Wild Garden* (1870)

championed a return to hardy plants, including foreign exotics capable of naturalizing in the garden.

By the 1870s the 'how to' gardening manuals of mid-century had given way to 'garden autobiographies'. The author was typically the garden owner, and a calendar recorded the seasonal face of their garden, with an occasional backward glance to a regrettable act of vandalism inflicted at the hands of a previous occupier. Personal recollections of scents and perfumes replaced debates over the 'correct' use of colour. And plants were recruited to record friendships while a sundial hinted at the unavoidable passage of time. All of these features were included in a garden created by Daisy Greville, Countess of Warwick, a decade before she brought Harold Peto in to work on her Easton Lodge Estate in Essex. Plants given by friends were labelled with pottery hearts identifying the giver to create a Garden of Friendship, while a Garden of Sentiment displayed pottery swallows, the wings of which recorded the name of each flower and an associated emblem researched in an appropriate-sounding 'bygone' text. This garden and the century were closing amid a strong scent of nostalgia.

Jane Bradney

Belsay Hall

Near Morpeth,
Northumberland
-
Sir Charles Monck
-
c. 1806–67
-
Registered Grade I

'I cut down the birch trees and planted up with seedling Oaks ...', so Sir Charles Monck recorded the planting up of Crag Wood's steep slopes to create the Quarry Garden around 1800. Although this is Belsay's most loved and valued garden, other areas from its long history contribute to Belsay's Grade I status – the early deer park, Bantam Hill *ferme ornée*, Crag Wood and two lakes from the 18th century and Monck's Terraced Gardens and Rhododendron Garden, all enclosed within parkland.

Belsay Castle, a tower house (or castle), was built in 1439–60. This was joined in 1614 by a manor house with formal gardens – Buck's 1728 drawing shows rectangular enclosures, walled from the surrounding fields and planted with topiary cones and balls, and railings on the south boundary. In the mid-18th century, a *ferme ornée* (a working farm but beautified) was laid out around the Home Farm, a folly on Bantam Hill. The folly was castellated (a real castle not enough, apparently) and given an impressive spire. Described In 1769 as '... Spire of the tempiato at Belsay ...', perhaps as an eyecatcher from the castle, it collapsed soon after it was built. Across the ground around the castle and the Bantam Hill folly, woods and parkland trees were planted, ha-has dug, walls, drives and bridges constructed, a massive terrace raised and an avenue planted (over-looking a stone-walled paddock for Belsay's stallions), a bath house built, the public road and village moved, and a large lake floated on the Coal Burn. Much of this landscape is lost, but many elements survive, buried in woodland or redundant in farmland.

OPPOSITE Working the quarry at Belsay created a number of different spaces.

Then, in 1795, Sir Charles Monck inherited and, following a Mediterranean honeymoon, decided to build a new house. The old castle and manor house were reduced to a steward's house, forming a romantic incident in the landscape. The new house (30 metres/100 foot square) was Greek Revival, with John Dobson involved in its construction. Quarries were opened to provide the stone.

Sir Charles's improvements covered all the core designed landscape at the Belsay estate. Ha-has, paths, steps and seats were added to the Crag Wood Oaks and a lake was made overlooked from the paths. A wide mix of trees, including many exotics, were planted throughout the landscape.

In 1831, his house finished, Sir Charles visited the ancient quarries at Syracuse, perhaps seeking ideas for his Belsay quarries. Initially these were appreciated for their bare cliffs and smooth rock surfaces – an undated 19th-century watercolour shows the quarries very largely unplanted; as the 19th century progressed, and perhaps particularly after 1867 when Sir Arthur Middleton, a noted plantsman, inherited, the quarries were gradually filled with exotic plant introductions. Today, there are glorious azaleas, rhododendrons, *Parrotia* and *Gunnera*.

Belsay Hall, Castle and Gardens have been managed by English Heritage since 1984. The terraces south of the hall were replanted in the 1990s to designs by Elizabeth Banks, and in 2022 by Dan Pearson. This process of regular renewal over 300 years ensures that all of Belsay's gardens continue to astonish and delight.

Nick Owen

Sheringham Park

Once seen, never forgotten – the dramatic view from the entrance drive of Sheringham Hall and park, embowered by a wooded hillside, framed by views of the sea. It is a view which you anticipate, if you are even slightly aware of the style of Sheringham's designer, Humphry Repton: the visitor passing through shady woods, before a signature sudden turn in the drive reveals the parkland panorama, in Repton's phrase 'bursting' on your sight.

Coming towards the end of his career in 1812, when he was working in partnership with his son John Adey, Repton declared Sheringham his favourite work. He found the place had 'more natural beauty and local advantages' than any he had ever seen; moreover his young clients, newly married Abbot and Charlotte Upcher, were his most congenial. The estate included a farming and fishing village, and was well connected by road and coastal waters to a wider world. Repton enhanced the landscape with an elegant house, park and pleasure grounds, new roads, drives, paths and estate buildings, as a structure for the good works the ardent Upchers envisioned in matters of social and scenic improvement.

The Upchers were delighted with the design and the Reptons continued to make site visits *con amore* to oversee its progress on the ground, but neither saw its completion. Abbot Upcher's early death in 1819 left the house a roofed shell, his widow remaining in a local farmhouse. It was left to the Upchers' son and heir Henry to complete the work from 1839, adding features, notably plantings of rare rhododendrons and azaleas, which attract so many visitors

Sheringham, Norfolk
-
Humphry and
John Adey Repton
-
1812–17
-
Registered Grade II*

OPPOSITE The hall 'bursts' into sight at a turn in the drive.

BELOW The view towards the sea.

LEFT The drive bordered by rhododendrons.

ABOVE Proposed view from the drive from Humphry Repton's Red Book for Sheringham (1812). The figure on the right sketching is Humphry Repton; the two on the left his clients Abbot and Charlotte Upcher.

now in the spring. The last Upcher of Sheringham, Thomas, inherited the estate in 1951, and made improvements that sought to restore Sheringham's Regency style, in the interior of the house as well as erecting a viewing temple that Repton planned but which had remained unbuilt.

In 1981, Sheringham was acquired by the National Trust, who have drawn on both the spirit and letter of Repton's Red Book of designs to manage the landscape. As Repton envisaged, the public have access to the park and its scenery, now with a gazebo giving panoramic views of the wider country, including sights of which Repton may well have approved: a smoke-trailing steam railway and offshore a fleet of modern windmills, the turbines of Sheringham Shoals.

Sheringham Hall and its pleasure grounds remain private, the present owners undertaking a careful, scholarly programme of work, restoring the house, conserving woodland walks and creating kitchen and ornamental gardens. It is a landscape for all seasons, to be lived in as well as looked at. In its rapport between Red Book and reality, synthesis of landscape and architecture, arrangement of private and public spaces, as well as its rich range of scenery, Sheringham is a fine place to appreciate Repton's mature art of landscape gardening. His client, Abbot Upcher, called it Repton's 'masterpiece' and many would agree.

Stephen Daniels

Endsleigh

Milton Abbott, Devon

–

Humphry Repton

–

1814

–

Registered Grade I

'Endsleigh Cottage is the most influential garden ever made in England'. Discuss.

Look out from the veranda at Endsleigh and blink; you could be in the hills above Poona, blink again and it's Nantucket, the outskirts of Johannesburg or Melbourne. The ripples of Endsleigh have spread, yet when he completed his design in 1814 Humphry Repton, who conceived both house and garden (though Jeffrey Wyatt detailed and executed the house), regarded himself as a failure. His grand ambition, to establish the principles of landscape creation, had come to nothing, so at Endsleigh he up-ended his rule book. Gone is the grand approach, sweeping through parkland and offering the choicest views to the visitor, with a climactic burst to the house. Endsleigh's approach runs through woodland, blind to the spectacular beauty of the Upper Tamar, and debouches at the back door, opposite the stables. The Scottish architect Sir Robert Lorimer would do the same with the stable yard at Glen House, Innerleithen (1905).

Far from representing to the world the standing of his client, the Duke of Bedford, the house is a cottage, its footprint a curve rather than a square, and so bent that having entered, the hall is dark; rather the book room offers a first view of the river – at the foot of a cow pasture beyond a little milking shed (the park, hitherto a staple of Reptonian design, has gone). Look for the return of the parterre and find it from the duchess's window, in perfection, enclosed by a long open passage, 90 years before the parterres of Rodmarton (1910).

The handling of the terracing behind the house, the long herbaceous border, the triangular lawn, the pergola, the summerhouse – there is nothing here that could not be seen at Kiftsgate (from 1920) or Snowshill or dozens of other Cotswold gardens, but this close integration of house and garden anticipates by 60 years William Morris's Arts and Crafts Movement, so visitors feel at home, and that makes the dingle, a short walk west of the cottage, a surprise.

OPPOSITE Repton's dramatic valley garden has year-round interest.

ABOVE Endsleigh is set in 44 hectares (108 acres) of gardens, woodlands, follies and grottos created by Humphry Repton.

The dingle is Repton's supreme achievement with water. It has a folly, the Dairy, but it is not about follies. It is surely a garden but it is not about flowers, statuary, terraces, *allées* or pergolas; it is less a garden than an immersive medium, like water, and above all the sound of water. Repton has led the water in channels on either side of this little valley and let if fall through a dozen rivulets down to the stream at the base, each one set naturally with rocks to give a peal of different sounds, base tenor and treble; trinkle, roar and boom. This is pure romance, saved from whimsy by its simplicity and its reliance on nature.

Endsleigh was little visited in Repton's lifetime. It owes its influence to Repton's final published work, for which his Endsleigh Red Book formed the 34th Fragment. Today it is a hotel, worthy of its reputation.

John Phibbs

Scotney Castle Gardens

As I open the gates at the castle, the clink of the latch resonates on the stone walls. From here, spellbound, I can trace Scotney's timeline through the garden. I follow the treeline to the canopies that cast dappled shade over the fossilized prehistoric seabed in the quarry. Out in the meadow beside the boathouse, where orchids, fritillaries and daffodils bejewel the grass, is the possible site of the first timber manor house built in the 1100s by the De Scoteni family.

In 1378 Roger de Ashburnham built the castle whose one remaining tower has become the iconic image of Scotney. We tend the lawns and borders that bloom where the great hall and chapel once stood. Dragonflies and swallows dart over the moat, and a kingfisher dives in for his morning catch, but in the 1500s there was a far louder splash when Jesuit priest Father Richard Blount made a daring escape as the castle was being searched. After hiding in the priest hole, he jumped out into the moat and swam to safety.

Only wisteria now climbs the old stairs to the grand front door of the ruins of the Palladian-style wing built in the 1630s by William Darell. The plants that frame the ruins form an idyllic scene: the roses round the window, the towering trees and billowing clouds of soft colour from the rhododendrons, the curve of path and lawn, and the wild flowers blooming from the steep-sided quarry. All these elements combine to create a stunning picture, which is no accident, and creates a feeling that as you stand and gaze you become part of all that surrounds you. Edward Hussey III wanted to redevelop the gardens and create a

Lamberhurst, Kent
-
William Sawrey Gilpin
-
1835
-
Registered Grade I

OPPOSITE View of the new house from the Old Castle bridge.

BELOW Lavender and roses bloom in the beds around the Old Castle.

new mansion following the principles of the Picturesque Movement. The intention was to unify the garden, the new mansion and the Old Castle, which was to be deliberately partially ruined, into a 'total work of art'.

On 10 November 1834, architect Anthony Salvin paid his first visit to Scotney. Two years later he, Edward and William Sawrey Gilpin agreed on the position of the new house. High on the hill, this house, built in the asymmetrical Tudor style that Salvin was noted for, is perfectly situated. From inside, the bay windows of the library and bedroom above act as picture frames for the castle deep in the valley.

Edward played an active role in the garden's development. His diaries reflect his passion and enthusiasm and he clearly had a great love for the place in which he built his new home and raised his family. His son, Edward Windsor Hussey, and in turn his nephew, Christopher Hussey, continued to nurture this unique garden. On Christopher's death he bequeathed Scotney to the National Trust. Today the garden is a Site of Special Scientific Interest and we look after rare species including dormice, great-crested newts and green-winged orchids.

What makes Scotney unforgettable for me, are the layers of history that create an enchanted feeling as you walk through the gardens, taking a trip back in time.

Andrea Bennett

OPPOSITE Fragrant herb beds surround a medieval Venetian well-head.

RIGHT Wisteria cascades over the staircase of the Old Castle ruins.

Sheffield Botanical Gardens

In the time before public parks, several provincial English towns established botanical gardens to provide recreation and education for the growing middle classes. One prominent example was to the south-west of industrialized Sheffield.

People gained the right of entry to the new gardens by purchasing shares in the organising society, which in turn funded the acquisition and laying out of the 7.5-hectare (18½-acre) site. An 1834 competition to find the best design was won by young Scottish landscape gardener Robert Marnock (1800–89). Leaving his role as head gardener at Bretton Hall, Marnock moved to Sheffield to oversee the creation of the gardens, and served as their curator for six years. He was to become one of the century's best-known designers and horticulturalists.

Marnock was supported in the design of the garden buildings by local architect Benjamin Broomhead Taylor (1806–48). Striking prospects were created within the sloping site and across neighbouring landscapes. On the high ground to the north, they built glass pavilions 90 metres (295 feet) long, consisting of three domed conservatories linked by glazed walkways (now listed Grade II*), alongside a classical gateway and Gothic Revival-style lodge to the south (both Grade II).

Still visible on the ground, the layout displays Marnock's characteristic mix of grand formal terraces and broad walks for promenading, surrounded by lawns, with more intimate paths winding gently among woodland, naturalistic ponds and artificial rockwork.

Sheffield,
South Yorkshire
-
Robert Marnock
-
1834–36
-
Registered Grade II

OPPOSITE The classical gateway to the gardens.

ABOVE A lithograph of the gardens, from a drawing by Isaac Shaw, 1850.

LEFT The restored pavilions and formal terrace.

OPPOSITE ABOVE Summer bedding in front of the south lodge.

OPPOSITE BELOW The bear pit, with sculpture by David Mayne.

Marnock quickly established impressive collections of woody and herbaceous plants. Many species had been recently introduced to England as a result of colonial trade, and were illustrated in *The Floricultural Magazine*, published by Marnock from 1836. The gardens are still renowned for their fine collection of trees, a few of which may be Marnock's plantings.

The gardens also included a selection of animals to amuse and educate visitors, most notably a black bear in its own pit and cages of monkeys, which delighted visiting schoolchildren. The animals disappeared after the gardening journalist J.C. Loudon opined that the repose of the gardens was being destroyed by their 'filth, stench, roaring, howling, and other annoyances'.

The new gardens were much praised but failed to become financially sustainable. In 1898 they were saved by the charitable Sheffield Town Trust, which paid off shareholders and opened the gardens to the public. The Trust extended the southern boundary and added new stone and wrought-iron entrance gates (Grade II), to attract working people from nearby mills and factories.

After an attack during the Blitz in 1941 damaged the pavilions, the city took over management and made repairs, but budget cuts later in the century saw the gardens decline. They were saved by a major restoration programme, completed in 2008, supported by a Heritage Fund grant of over £5 million.

The gardens are still owned by the Town Trust and managed by Sheffield City Council. They boast a dedicated education centre and are supported by volunteer gardeners, a Friends group and a charitable trust. With the restored pavilions seen by many as a symbol of Sheffield, the gardens are open free to the public all year.

Jill Sinclair

Westonbirt Gardens

Across the road from the world-famous arboretum lies the lesser-known but equally unforgettable garden and park of Westonbirt. The garden remains almost unchanged from its original conception, which landowner and MP Robert Stayner Holford (1808–92) planned 20 years before he built his new mansion. The park, arboretum and house were developed as part of a single grand design, strongly influenced by William Sawrey Gilpin, on picturesque principles for laying out grounds. Some of the trees and shrubs represent their first introductions to Britain. Holford created a garden which fused science, art, architecture and inspired arboriculture.

The Westonbirt estate had been in the Holford family since 1685, but they had mainly been absentee landlords until 1811, when they built a new gothic-style villa on the site of the current mansion. The Holfords were fabulously rich from legal work, good investments and fortuitous marriages.

Robert Holford left Oxford in 1829 and began planting Westonbirt Arboretum. In 1839 he inherited the estate and began work on the eastern, Italianate, architecturally led end of the garden: the rockery (now the fernery), kitchen gardens, hothouses and Mercury and Italian gardens, most of which date from 1843 onwards. Lewis Vulliamy, who later created the house and lodges, designed the structures. Holford extended his passion for tree planting into the new parkland. Lists of trees he purchased are recorded in his notebooks, collated by his long-serving head gardener Jonah Neale.

In the mid-1850s the old village was demolished and a new one built further west, and new entrance lodges

Easton Grey,
Near Tetbury,
Gloucestershire

–

Robert Stayner
Holford

–

1839–74

–

Registered Grade I

OPPOSITE The Camellia House, rebuilt by Sir George Lindsay Holford in 1910.

BELOW An undated photograph of pupils having lessons in the Italian Garden.

completed. Once this was underway, the more informal western side of the garden was developed, with its lake and grotto of Pulhamite stone (1873–4). As well as specimen trees, other groups of one or two tall trees surrounded by smaller ones with varied colours, exemplify Holford's interest in botanical novelty and plant grouping.

In 1864 he commissioned a new mansion by Lewis Vulliamy to replace the villa. Completed in 1872 at a cost of £200,000, this was one of the most expensive houses of the century, fitted with the newest technology: gas lighting, central heating, fireproof construction and iron roofs.

Holford lived and breathed his creation at Westonbirt for 53 years until he died in 1892. His son George Lindsay Holford further developed the gardens and extended the acer collection and orchid cultivation. He redeveloped the glasshouses, and rebuilt the Camellia House around 1910. As he was childless, the estate was sold on his death in 1926 and the estate became a school. The arboretum passed to the Forestry Commission in 1956 in lieu of death duties.

In 2006 The Holfords of Westonbirt Trust was founded to enable the long-term conservation of the house and gardens and to make them accessible to a wider audience. The trust's most recent project has seen the repair and refurbishment of many of the garden's most important historic features, including the lake and the Italian Garden. Completed in 2021, the works were funded by a combination of grant aid and private donations.

Margie Hoffnung

Derby Arboretum

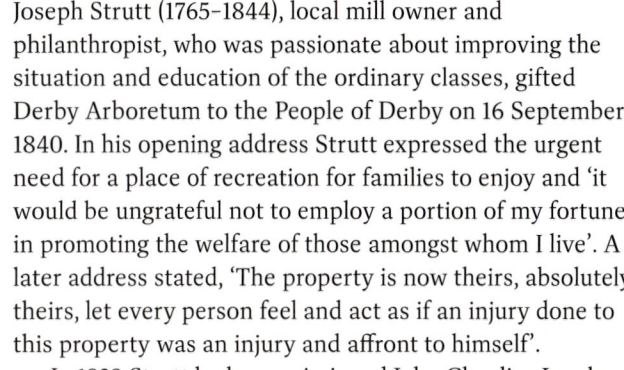

Arboretum Square, Derby

–

John Claudius Loudon

–

1840

–

Registered Grade II*

Joseph Strutt (1765–1844), local mill owner and philanthropist, who was passionate about improving the situation and education of the ordinary classes, gifted Derby Arboretum to the People of Derby on 16 September 1840. In his opening address Strutt expressed the urgent need for a place of recreation for families to enjoy and 'it would be ungrateful not to employ a portion of my fortune in promoting the welfare of those amongst whom I live'. A later address stated, 'The property is now theirs, absolutely theirs, let every person feel and act as if an injury done to this property was an injury and affront to himself'.

In 1839 Strutt had commissioned John Claudius Loudon (1783–1843), arguably Britain's foremost landscape gardener of his time, to design 'a place of recreation for the inhabitants of Derby and for all' stipulating, 'that it should be open (free of charge) a minimum two days a week, one to be Sunday.'

Loudon's initial observations of the site were that 'the surface is flat, apparently level' and 'particularly well adapted for the growth of trees'. Contrary to Strutt's initial request for a botanic garden, Loudon argued the case for an Arboretum and produced a design that would maximize the appeal of the 4.5-hectare (11-acre) site. Loudon's primary arguments in favour of an arboretum were that to enjoy their beauties, herbaceous plants being small and low 'would soon, instead of a recreation, become very fatiguing' and that the sources of interest of trees and shrubs from 'the opening buds in spring', 'the intensely deep green of summer' to the 'first changes of autumn to red or yellow' would be of greater enjoyment.

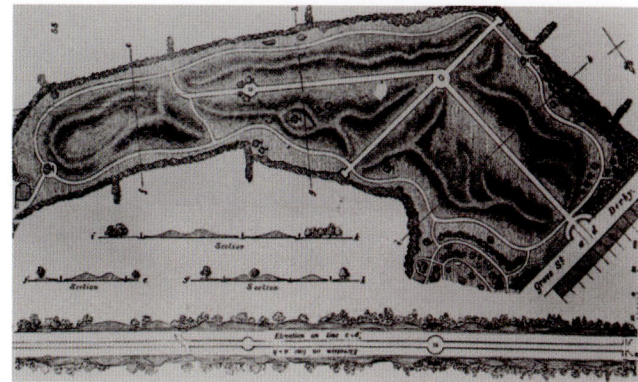

Incorporated into the plan was a complex series of beautifully undulating mounds, the purposes of which were primarily to show trees to their best advantage and to obscure sight lines between paths and to boundaries, increasing the scale of the garden. Loudon stated that to display a tree without the ramification of its roots structure visible would be 'Contrary to truth, nature and health of the tree' and was a 'monstrous and unnatural appearance.'

Loudon also incorporated pathways, particularly a serpentine path around the boundary, further increasing the sense of scale, with further straight paths intersecting at the central seating area where the fountain (1850) now stands. Further consideration regarding the paths was that they should have a distinct reason for terminating, to which end two lodges (E.B. Lamb 1806–9), two pavilions, the Florentine Boar and planted urns were incorporated into the design to act as points of destination for people to enjoy as they walked around.

Derby Arboretum should be considered as the physical outpouring of Loudon's 1838 publication *Arboretum et fruticetum Britannicum*. Laid out in his Gardenesque style, originally 913 trees and shrubs were displayed taxonomically in family groups, labelled, and spaced so that 'every plant is allowed to grow as in its native habitat'. Restored with Heritage Lottery Funding, and completed in 2005, Derby Arboretum continues to be managed in accordance with Loudon's and Strutt's original intentions.

Michael J. McNaught

Abney Park Cemetery

On the west side of Stoke Newington High Street, sandwiched between a row of shops and a row of houses, is an impressive Egyptian-style gateway. Once past the gates, the visitor takes a path between boundary walls until the cemetery opens out, revealing a thick woodland punctuated by monuments. It was, of course, not planned as a woodland – the woods are mostly self-seeded, the result of mid-20th-century neglect – but it was planned as a garden.

Abney Park Cemetery was opened in 1840, as part of the wave of cemetery-making that began in the 1820s. Like its predecessors in London (Kensal Green, Norwood and Highgate), it advertised itself as open for all denominations; but unlike those, it contained no consecrated ground, so few Anglicans availed themselves of its services. Basically a cemetery for Dissenters, its site was chosen because of its associations with the most famous of Dissenting hymn-writers, Isaac Watts, who had lived at Abney Park House for a quarter-century and planted trees there. He is commemorated by a massive statue by E.H. Baily, in the middle of a central path. The Dissenting connection pervades the cemetery: William Booth, the founder of the Salvation Army, is buried alongside his family and other prominent members, and nearby is the obelisk of Thomas Binney, the Congregationalist minister and anti-slavery campaigner.

Abney Park had only one chapel, theoretically open for all denominations to use. It was designed by the architect William Hosking, who seems to have thought that this diversity of clientele justified an eclectic building style.

Stoke Newington High Street, London Borough of Hackney

–

William Hosking; George Loddiges

–

1840

RIGHT Mid-20th-century neglect has turned one of the paths in Abney Park into a woodland walk.

LEFT E.H. Baily's statue of Isaac Watts, erected by public subscription in 1845.

BELOW LEFT An angel, on the grave of Elizabeth Armsworth (d. 1916), wife of a Hackney newsagent.

The cruciform brick chapel has 14th-century, 15th-century and Romanesque detailing on different fronts. The other main architectural feature inside the grounds is a 1920s war memorial, in the form of a raised terrace over some of the now closed catacombs; it is surmounted by the Reginald Blomfield Cross of Sacrifice.

The landscaping of the cemetery was in large part the work of George Loddiges, who had succeeded his father Conrad as director of the Loddiges Nursery in Hackney, probably the most prestigious nursery of its day, with what were then the world's largest glasshouses. Many of the estate's original trees were retained, with a yew walk created out of a grove; some 2,000 varieties were added, the trees carrying identifying labels to help educate the public about botany. Portions of the site not initially used for burial were turned into ornamental gardens: an 'American garden' of shrubs requiring peaty soil, like rhododendrons and kalmias, and a 'rosarium' with 1,029 named varieties. (George Collison's book *Cemetery Interment*, published the year the cemetery opened, provided complete lists.) These gardens vanished as the land filled with graves.

The Abney Park Cemetery Company flourished for nearly a century, opening or acquiring other cemeteries in London; but eventually it lurched towards bankruptcy. In 1974, the deterioration of the cemetery spurred the creation of Save Abney Park Cemetery, which persuaded Hackney Council to take the cemetery over in 1979. Since then there have been programmes of repair, culminating in the current restoration of the chapel.

Brent Elliott

Shrubland Hall

BELOW View of the garden front of Shrubland Hall with new steps and terraces. From *The Life and Works of Sir Charles Barry*, 1867.

Coddenham, Suffolk

–

Donald Beaton, Anne Middleton; Charles Barry

–

1830s–1850s

–

Registered Grade I

The gardens at Shrubland Hall are laid out around a steep slope forming the eastern side of the Gipping Valley. In the 17th century, the manor house, set back from the top of the slope, was accompanied by an enclosed garden, a small deer park and – extending down the slope – an area called The Warren, densely planted with sweet chestnuts. In the 1770s, John Bacon built a compact Palladian house, designed by James Paine, on a new site, some 0.5 kilometres (⅓ mile) to the south-west of what became the 'old' hall, on the edge of the escarpment. A gothic prospect tower was erected around 0.7 kilometres (⅖ mile) to the north-east and a landscape park created. Humphry Repton prepared a Red Book for the site in 1789 and while some of his proposals - relating to a new approach to the house from the south - were implemented, most were not.

Shrubland has an important early history but its real glory is its 19th-century gardens. William Fowle Middleton, 2nd Baronet (1784–1860) inherited in 1830 and commissioned J.P. Gandy Deering to expand and remodel the house in loosely Italianate style. Through the 1830s and 1840s, a remarkable series of gardens was created by head gardener, Donald Beaton, and Middleton's wife Anne (neé Cust). These were mainly laid out along the 0.75-kilometre (½-mile) long, ruler-straight Green Terrace at the foot of the slope, below the house. They included the French Garden, a parterre with marble busts enclosed by a laurel hedge; the Fountain Garden, with a curved heated wall and 30 radiating beds, where Beaton experimented with the organization of colour in bedding-out schemes; and the Chinese Garden,

'with its large hanging baskets suspended on poles, its quaint groundwork of tiles, scrolled beds of box and silver sand filled mostly with sweet-centred pelargoniums and embellished with Irish junipers' (*Gardeners' Chronicle*, 1868). Towards the southern end of the Green Terrace were a box maze and the Swiss Garden, with rockeries and full-sized chalet. All this was initially connected to the house, and the balustraded Balcony Garden beside it, by paths running up the slope. But in 1852 Charles Barry, who had been employed to make further changes to the house, implemented Anne Middleton's idea for a monumental 'Villa d'Este descent'. This comprised a magnificent flight of stone steps, axially aligned on the house, running down the slope from Balcony Garden to Green Terrace. Here it terminated at the Panel Garden, with parterres and Loggia. Through the 1850s the park was expanded, remodelled and given a series of impressive lodges.

Renowned when first created, the gardens were progressively simplified from the 1880s, but were well maintained even after the hall became a health resort in 1965. In 2008 the property was sold and the park divided. The gardens are no longer regularly opened to the public and their condition has deteriorated, but the main elements – Balcony Garden, Descent, Panel Garden, Green Terrace, Fountain Garden, Swiss Garden and maze – all survive. So too does the park, complete with prospect tower and the ancient chestnuts of The Warren. Shrubland remains a magical place.

Tom Williamson

Biddulph Grange

OPPOSITE The Italian Garden with its stepped terraces and balustrades.

BELOW The Egyptian Court.

Biddulph, Staffordshire

–

James Bateman and Edward Cooke

–

1840

–

Registered Grade I

The Batemans, wealthy Salford industrialists, purchased the Knypersley Hall estate on the west facing slopes of Biddulph Moor in the 1780s, primarily for its coal and mineral resources. John Bateman remodelled and extended the house and garden. In the 1830s his son James, well respected in plant-collecting circles since his undergraduate days at Oxford, worked on the design, making considerable use of monolithic blocks of local stone.

In 1840, James and his wife Maria, settled at the northern end of the estate. They began to remodel an existing house and create a new garden. The marine artist and garden designer Edward Cooke visited in 1847 and an immediate friendship was formed. Drawing on his experience of painting and garden design featuring rockwork, Cooke assisted Bateman in reshaping 8.5 hectares (21 acres) of unpromising hill slope, using mounding and the clever placing of large pieces of stone to create a series of discrete interconnected but not intervisible compartments. Each garden has its own theme. China, entered through the Stumpery, a collection of upturned tree roots embedded in a bank, is surrounded by the Great Wall. Within lies a mock tea temple and wooden bridge over the pool, all overlooked by a watch tower and mock pagoda. The Fernery sits in a steep-sided glen astride a stream; the Egyptian Court is guarded by two sphinxes, flanked by topiary yew hedges leading to a pyramidal portico. There is a quoit ground, an arboretum and a very formal dahlia walk. Each compartment had its own microclimate suitable for the complementary

themed planting, much of which was of individual species introduced to Great Britain for the first time. Although the layout was created with great seriousness, Bateman and Cooke had a mischievous sense of fun and surprise. A dark twisting tunnel from the Fernery emerges into the Chinese Temple; a replica of the Ape of Thoth lurks in a dark recess in the Egyptian pavilion ready to startle the unwary, before a staircase ascends into a replica half-timbered Cheshire Cottage, the terminal feature of the Pinetum.

Bateman's south-facing mansion house (largely rebuilt after a fire in 1896) stood on a terrace overlooking a small pool and the Rhododendron Ground. The line of the terrace continues east, through the Wellingtonia Avenue into the wider park and up towards the moors where the perspective of a steep gradient and the silver sandy finish of the tree-lined path still give the illusion of an obelisk. Visitors originally entered the gardens through the Geological Gallery in which Bateman, an Evangelical Christian, attempted to reconcile the Biblical story of Creation with the new Darwinian theories of evolution through a seven-day geological timeline formed with original rocks and fossils.

After Bateman left Biddulph in 1871 the property passed through several ownerships before becoming an orthopaedic hospital. The gardens suffered from neglect and vandalism before they were acquired by the National Trust in 1988, opening to the public in 1992: the wider parkland became a local authority country park.

Alan Taylor

Birkenhead Park

Park Drive,
Birkenhead,
Merseyside

–

Joseph Paxton

–

Opened April 1847

–

Registered Grade I

Most of the 27,000 public parks in the UK – aside from some funded by public subscription or wealthy benefactors – were created by local authorities, following the Select Committee for Public Walks in 1833 and the Public Health Act of 1875. Birkenhead was the first public park to be established at public expense in the country and had a major impact both nationally and internationally.

Yet it is the ingenuity of the innovative design of Joseph Paxton (1803–65) that makes this place so special. Paxton was born at Milton Bryan in Bedfordshire, and was head gardener for the Duke of Devonshire at Chatsworth from 1826. He took on a vast array of other projects, including many public parks, but his biographer George F. Chadwick states that 'Paxton's most important public park, at any rate in its influence in relation to the development of the movement for public parks both in this country and elsewhere, was that at Birkenhead.'

While Sir William Jackson is often credited with establishing Birkenhead Park, it is Mr Isaac Holmes, a Liverpool councillor representing the interests of the city on the Birkenhead Improvement Commission, who suggested to his fellow commissioners that they should investigate the possibility of developing a public park in the town. Two years later his suggestion was realized when Parliament passed the town's second Improvement Act which empowered the commissioners to purchase land for a park. Sir William Jackson was the chairman of the new Improvement Committee, and he approached Paxton to ascertain what he would charge for designing it.

OPPOSITE Birkenhead
Park boat house.

LEFT A young Joseph
Paxton, 1851.

According to C.E. Thornton's history of the park, there were concerns about whether the site was suitable for a public park, being 'so poor, a mixture of fields, marsh and common'. Despite this, Paxton's plan was approved by the commissioners. He employed two assistants to help with the works, John Robertson, an architectural assistant from Chatsworth, and Edward Kemp, who moved to Birkenhead to supervise the works. The park was eventually opened on 10 April 1847. When H. Gawthrop, author of *The Mersey and the Ferries*, visited in 1853, he described how 'here nature may be viewed in her lovliest [sic] garb – the most obdurate heart may be softened, and the mind led to pursuits which refine and alleviate the humblest of the toil-worn'.

One of the most innovative aspects of Paxton's design was its circulation pattern, with the separation of traffic. 'Pleasure traffic' was restricted to the perimeter carriage drive while 'within the park are the footpaths, linking all parts and with convenient connections to the outside traffic roads'. This deeply impressed Frederick Law Olmsted when he visited in 1852 and in 1858, when he was designing Central Park, New York, and it is echoed in his work there.

Birkenhead Park has stood the test of time. It remains internationally important, an inspiration for the many who visit today and testament to the genius of Joseph Paxton.

Paul Rabbitts

ABOVE The Swiss Bridge, Birkenhead Park.

ABOVE RIGHT The Italian Lodge, Birkenhead Park, c. 1843–47, by Lewis Hornblower and John Robertson.

RIGHT A vintage postcard featuring the Swiss Bridge.

THE PARK, BIRKENHEAD.

Old Town Cemetery, Stirling

The plateau below Stirling Castle had been used as a tilting ground and a fairground before the 1850s, when it was turned into a cemetery. The idea came from Charles Rogers (1825–90), the chaplain of the castle garrison, in collaboration with William Drummond (1793–1888), a wealthy nurseryman who had also opened an agricultural museum in Stirling.

The architects were John Dick Peddie (1824–91) and Charles Kinnear (1830–94).

The main body of the cemetery, now called the Valley Cemetery, occupies a level ground framed by rocky outcrops, including one called the Ladies' Rock because it was supposed to have provided seating for ladies watching the events below. On the opposite side, a few years after the cemetery's opening, Drummond created an ornamental garden, incorporating a fishpond (an unusual feature for a cemetery in those days); this is now called Drummond's Garden.

But the cemetery had a second purpose, beyond a place of burial for the dead. It was also conceived as a celebration of Scottish Nonconformity, with a series of statues of the heroes of the Reformers, and in particular the Covenanters, the group that in 1638 signed a covenant opposing the attempts of Charles I to impose a single church on England and Scotland. In the 1660s, Charles II renewed his father's campaign, expelling hundreds of ministers and imposing heavy punishments on any who refused to abjure the covenant; the 1680s became known as the 'killing time' because of the number of executions, before the ousting of James II allowed the Scots' Church.

Below Stirling Castle

-

William Drummond; Charles Rogers

-

Opened 1857

OPPOSITE The cemetery today.

BELOW A photograph of the cemetery taken from the Ladies' Rock, sometime between 1863 and 1867.

The sculptor Handyside Ritchie (1804–70) was commissioned to carve statues of John Knox (c. 1514–72), the founder of the Church of Scotland, and Andrew Melville (1545–1622) and Alexander Henderson (c. 1583–1646), the pioneering Covenanters. These three figures stand on an outcrop that provides the central feature of the Valley Cemetery. Further statues of Reverend James Guthrie (c. 1612–61) and James Renwick (1662–88), the first and last of the Covenanters hanged for treason, and Ebenezer Erskine (1680–1754), the founder of the Secession Church, are placed in roundabouts elsewhere. A few years later, Ritchie added a statue in marble, of the Wigtown martyrs, Margaret MacLachlan and Margaret Wilson, two Covenanters who were drowned in 1685; this statue is covered by a tall glass dome to protect the marble from erosion.

The religious theme was continued in an immense stone pyramid at the top of the cemetery, dedicated to religious martyrs generally. Its four sides bear curious inscriptions ('The light of the star', 'The anthem of grace'), which were in fact the titles of religious tracts printed by Drummond's brother and then available for sale in the town. A little distance to the left of the pyramid is Drummond's own grave, the most elevated in the cemetery, looking down on his creation.

The cemetery gradually expanded, until the boundary between it and the old kirkyard was effaced. More recently, improved signage and railings have made the demarcations apparent, and although Drummond's Pleasure Ground is gated, the pyramid and Drummond's grave are normally accessible to visitors.

Brent Elliott

Inverewe

Wester Ross

–

Osgood Hanbury
Mackenzie;
Mairi Sawyer

–

1863

–

Listed in Historic
Environment
Scotland's Inventory
of Gardens and
Designed Landscapes

BELOW Overlooking
the Walled Garden.

A visit to Inverewe has always been unforgettable, beginning with the dramatic and beautiful journey to get there, between rugged mountains, over empty moorland and beside wild, dark lochs. Arriving over the hill at Poolewe to a view of the sea feels like bursting into light, and the first glimpse of the rugged headland of Inverewe ahead intrigues; could those possibly be palms, growing here?

Inverewe grew from the bold vision of Osgood Mackenzie to develop a garden on an exposed coastal promontory in the North West Highlands, where the only plants noted were two dwarf willows (*Salix herbacea*). Gifted the land at age 20, he left his mother to see to building his house, Osgood's priority being to establish a productive garden. He commissioned major engineering works of terracing and wall-building, creating a high, curved, south-facing amphitheatre just above the rocky shoreline. This walled garden was soon growing more than just food for the table – within 20 years *The Times* records it also being home to rare creepers and luxuriant myrtles (*Myrtus*).

Osgood also quickly set to planting trees, having first fenced the peninsula to keep sheep out. He used local provenance Scots pine (*Pinus sylvestris*) and oaks initially, but by the 1880s he was diversifying, also adding Corsican pine (*P. nigra*) as shelter. Subsequent thinning created protected 'enclosures', thereby maximizing the benefit of the warming North Atlantic Drift, where exotic trees, shrubs and other plants could be introduced. Osgood was developing relationships with other garden owners and botanic gardens and was travelling widely, inspired by the flora of

LEFT Woodland Garden
with its sheltering trees.

BELOW LEFT Mairi
Sawyer making the gift of
Inverewe to the National
Trust for Scotland in
1952.

OPPOSITE The Walled
Garden at Inverewe.

other countries and swapping plant material. People were interested in his experience, and he wrote many articles on plants and on growing in such an extreme location. He had married, and his only daughter, Mairi, travelled with him and shared his passion for plants and gardening.

When Osgood died in 1922, Mairi was living nearby with her husband. She inherited Osgood's estate, but did not actually move into the garden until 1937 when a new villa was built on the site of the first house, which had burnt down in 1914. However, she actively continued to care for the garden throughout her life, taking a very hands-on approach. Mairi is specifically credited with the development of the ponds in the garden, peat banks, the rock garden in front of the house and the planting of Coronation Knoll. She could see how interested people were in the sheer achievement of Inverewe, regularly welcoming visitors and opening the garden for charity. Her decision to transfer ownership to the National Trust for Scotland in 1952 secured the garden for visitors for the future.

We owe so much to Osgood Mackenzie for his pioneering vision, and to Mairi Sawyer for carrying that forward in spirit, adding her own interpretation. And we are indebted to the nine head gardeners and their teams who have followed in their footsteps, balancing experimentation with beauty and heritage, while always keeping a steady eye on the future, planning for the long-term health and resilience of this unforgettable garden.

Ann Steele

Avenham and Miller Parks

Preston, Lancashire
–
Edward Milner
–
1864–67
–
Registered Grade II*

Avenham and Miller Parks are effectively a single park, bisected by a railway line on an embankment. They were laid out on what had long been a beauty spot, the steep scarp above the River Ribble, at the top of which is the city's edge, marked by Georgian and Victorian houses sited to command the view south into the adjoining countryside. A promenade, Avenham Walk, had been built in the 17th century, described by the antiquarian Ralph Thoresby in 1702 as 'a very curious walk and delicate prospect'. Later, a commercial pleasure garden was established by a Mr Charles Jackson, which Preston Corporation bought in 1844 as it began to recognize the need to secure the land for public amenity.

The parks were designed by Edward Milner (1819–84), who learnt his trade as an apprentice at Chatsworth under Joseph Paxton, and then acted as Paxton's foreman at Prince's Park Liverpool and later the People's Park in Halifax. His proposal was presented to the corporation in 1864 and the parks were opened in 1867.

They are quite different in character: Avenham with its serpentine walks along the high ground looking down through trees on a grassy amphitheatre and the tree-lined river; Miller Park with its broad Italianate terrace, balustrade, staircase, urns and tazzas (shallow bowls on pedestals) and a large, formal fountain and pool as the focal point below. The planting in Miller Park especially exemplified Milner's mid-Victorian picturesque ideal: elaborate shrub beds characterized by graded planting around intricate bays, promontories and islands.

OPPOSITE A statue of Edward Geoffrey Stanley, 14th Earl of Derby, looks out over the Italianate terrace at Miller Park.

The development of public parks is entwined with
industrial and urban expansion. Preston's parks were an
integral part of its development from a small market town
to an industrial powerhouse; monuments to a place forging
a new identity. That entanglement is exemplified by the
parks' relationship to the railway: they are separated by
the embankment on which the East Lancashire Railway
was built, and bounded on one side by a tramway, later
incorporated into the park, and on the other by the
mainline approach to Preston Station. The banks were
carefully and extensively landscaped, the mainline in
particular was elaborately ornamented with one of Pulham
and Son's most remarkable creations in artificial stone –
cliffs, arches, stairways, cascades and pools, all exquisitely
softened by vegetation in purpose-built planting pockets,
and the whole confection topped by passing trains.

And at Preston you can see why parks remain a vital
part of the urban realm. The council was quick off the mark
in applying for National Lottery-funding and benefited
from substantial sums to pay for repairs to infrastructure,
architectural features and historic planting, as well as a new
riverside pavilion. As a result, the parks remain enormously
popular and an integral part of the life of the city, the
venue for events and activities large and small, and offering
beautiful walks and those views of the countryside, only five
minutes from Fishergate, the bustling main street of the city.

David Lambert

Waddesdon Manor

Waddesdon, Buckinghamshire

–

Baron Ferdinand de Rothschild assisted by Elie Lainé

–

1874–1922

–

Registered Grade I

In 1874 Baron Ferdinand de Rothschild (1839–98) bought 1,093 hectares (2,700 acres) of farmland from the Duke of Marlborough with a view to creating his own estate, close to where other members of the Rothschild family had settled some years earlier (at Tring and Mentmore). Born in Frankfurt and raised on the continent, Baron Ferdinand was a prominent member of the international Jewish banking dynasty and a passionate art collector, later to become a Liberal MP.

Baron Ferdinand employed the French architect Hippolyte Destailleur to build a mansion in the style of a 16th-century French château at the top of an eminent outcrop, Lodge Hill. The Parisian landscape gardener Elie Lainé (1829–1911) was subsequently called in to help with the outlines of the surrounding park, its drives and plantations. The adjoining pleasure grounds and gardens however, were 'laid out by my bailiff and gardener according to my notions and under my superintendence' (Ferdinand de Rothschild in his Red Book, 1897).

The baron filled his house with English 18th-century pictures, furniture and decorative arts (largely French in origin) and Parisian panelling; similarly, he furnished the gardens with 17th- and 18th-century French and Italian sculpture and other ornaments. The planting, however, was distinctly Victorian, with formal parterres with colourful bedding schemes. The firm of James Pulham and Sons was entrusted with the construction of much ornamental rockwork, notably a large rock garden just below a vast range of display glasshouses. An aviary and an ornamental

dairy had their own garden settings. Herbaceous borders and rose beds, and a long fruit wall, were laid out at the bottom of the hill, together with a large kitchen garden.

Baron Ferdinand died in 1898, leaving Waddesdon Manor to his sister, Miss Alice de Rothschild (1847–1922). Under Alice's guidance the gardens reached their zenith, as illustrated in a unique series of early colour autochromes of c. 1912.

Alice died in 1922, leaving Waddesdon to her great-nephew, James de Rothschild (1878–1957) and his wife Dorothy (1895–1988). They saw the property through the depression of the 1930s and the Second World War, during which the gardens were much simplified. While the manor and adjacent pleasure gardens were bequeathed to the National Trust in 1957 and opened to visitors, the dairy garden, glasshouses and rock garden were not part of the public areas and gradually fell into disrepair.

When Lord Rothschild (1936–2024) inherited the wider Waddesdon estate in 1988, he also took over as the chairman of what is now the Rothschild Foundation, which runs Waddesdon on behalf of the National Trust. He immediately instigated an extensive program of restoration. This focused on the manor and gardens and included the reinstatement of the original Victorian bedding schemes. Both the aviary and dairy were restored (the aviary continues to house a living collection of rare and endangered birds) with their original garden settings, while the rock garden was redeveloped by Isabel and Julian Bannerman. Today the gardens also display various pieces of contemporary sculpture, acquired by the Rothschild Foundation, and are open to the public.

Sophie Piebenga

ABOVE Built in 1889, the aviary would have been filled with colourful and exotic birds.

RIGHT Ornamental beds in the parterre garden.

Leonardslee Lakes and Gardens

Leonardslee is a gloriously dramatic landscape stretching across a forest ridge, traversed by a belt of seven historic ponds. Fostered by microclimates, Sir Edmund Loder (1849–1920) planted a world of trees and plants (over 10,000 have been catalogued) which paint a living picture that excites the eye and invites exploration by botanists and families alike. Beyond, and interrelated, was the planting of nearby High Beeches and Wakehurst Place. His name is famed among collectors of rhododendrons, azaleas, camellias, magnolias and acers; Sir Edmund also collected exotic conifers and today Leonardslee is closely associated with the International Conifer Conservation Programme.

Sir Edmund ran the estate until his death in 1920. His son Robert had been killed in the First World War, so his widow Muriel managed the estate until 1945, when her son Giles took over with his wife Marie (née Symons-Jeune, daughter of the noted landscape designer Bertram). Soon after their younger son Robin Loder inherited in 1981, the plantings were devastated by the 1987 storm, and the gardens closed in 2010. In 2017, Penny Streeter acquired first the landscape and then the mansion.

A contemporary Crystal Palace leads you onto a gentle winding path towards the Italianate mansion and upper gardens. The extensive Pulhamite Rock Garden has a network of paths and water features, with abundant colourful evergreen Japanese Kurume azaleas, originally introduced by E.H. 'Chinese' Wilson. The Camellia Walk, exotically interspersed with palm trees, includes the blood-red *Camellia* 'Takanini' bred in New Zealand,

Horsham,
West Sussex
-
Sir Edmund Loder
-
Created from 1889
onwards
-
Registered Grade I

OPPOSITE This aerial view shows part of the series of lakes running along a north–south belt at Leonardslee that originally served its ironworks.

Rhododendron stenopetalum 'Linearifolium', and *Pieris* species, including the vividly red-leaved *P. formosa* 'Wakehurst'. The newly planted Pinotage vineyard (the UK's first) traces 16 hectares (40 acres) of the undulating landscape as you journey down towards the ponds through trees, many of which have Champion status, and shrub-filled slopes, pausing to imbibe views that stretch to the coast on a clear day. The Head Lake, crossed by the Clapper Bridge, feeds a north–south belt from Top Ponds to Mossy Ghyll Pond – shaded by two oaks, the Hungarian or Italian oak, *Quercus frainetto* and the Macedonian oak, *Q. trojana* – and then the Engine Pond. Up above these ponds is the Upper Dell where some of the oldest plants grow: mature rhododendrons such as the Exbury hybrid 'Golden Dream', the large flowered 'White Glory' as well as one of the country's largest *Magnolia campbellii*, and original dawn redwoods, *Metasequoia glyptostroboides*. Waterfall Pond finally leads to New Pond. In 1952 a Coronation Garden had been created with younger specimens of all the Loderii rhododendron hybrids. In 2022 restoration work started and *Magnolia stellata* 'Royal Star' was planted for Charles III.

There are many trails across the 97-hectare (240-acre) landscape, a plantsman's dream skilfully tended by Jamie Harris and a team of 14 gardeners, now recarpeted with 50,000 snowdrops and 100,000 early narcissus. In 2021 living colour and scent were joined by a changing artistic scene initiated by a display of Anton Smit bronze sculptures. Apart from their plant nursery, wine and food outlets are inspired by and use Leonardslee fruits and leaves.

Caroline Holmes

Athelhampton

Dorchester, Dorset

Francis Inigo Thomas

1891

Registered Grade I

OPPOSITE The view into
the Corona garden.

BELOW The Great Court
with parterre and two
young pyramidal yews.

Architect Francis Inigo Thomas (1865-1950) was 26 years old and working with Reginald Blomfield (1856-1942) on their book *The Formal Garden* when he was commissioned to redesign the house and create the gardens at Athelhampton. Athelhampton Hall lies 10 kilometres (6 miles) north-east of Dorchester, in the valley of the River Piddle. Since 1485 the house had belonged to a succession of owners until, in 1891, it was acquired by wealthy gentleman Alfred Cart de Lafontaine (1865-1944). Thomas Hardy (1840-1928), who had been born nearby, was a regular visitor.

Athelhampton's gardens consist of the original garden rooms designed by Thomas, and 20th-century additions by Thomas Mawson (1861-1933), Sir Robert Cooke MP (1930-87) and Sir Harold Hillier (1905-85), fashioned in keeping with the spirit of the original design.

Thomas's vision was picturesque and poetic, yet architectural. His garden was regular although not symmetrical. Axes respected the layout of the house, but colour and fragrance were of great importance as was water, although the River Piddle itself was not incorporated into the design. Architectural, formal features such as terraces, balustrades, summerhouses, sundial, fountains, niches, obelisks and wrought-iron gates were vital and striking elements.

Thomas's garden enclosures and their contents represent the public face of Athelhampton today. The Great Court was planted with 12 pyramidal yews and geometric flower beds edged with box. Today the flowers have had to make way for these memorable giant yew which reach a

height of about 10 metres (30 feet). Overlooking the Great
Court is a terrace flanked by two stone pavilions, each
embellished with a carved face representing summer (joy)
and winter (unhappiness) respectively. From the Great
Court steps descend through an imposing but intricate
wrought-iron gate into the circular Corona garden, enclosed
by a scalloped stone wall surmounted by obelisks. Thomas's
design positioned a sundial at its centre, but a circular
pond and fountain replaced it. The Corona garden leads
to the Private Garden, also enclosed, and flanked by the
house itself at one end, with lawn and a sunken rectangular
pool with apsidal ends. Another arch leads to the smaller,
enclosed Lion's Mouth garden, from where two stone
archways lead into the Lime Walk.

Beyond these areas are the 20th-century additions: a
yew walk designed by Thomas Mawson, a White Garden,
a Rose Garden, an octagonal Cloister Garden with a
double row of pleached limes and a canal encased with
lawn and *Magnolia grandiflora*, created in 1971. A kitchen
garden, constructed between 1902 and 1918, is enclosed
by brick walls, and contains early 20th-century glass
houses, a central pool and fountain. Giles Keating acquired
Athelhampton in 2019.

Athelhampton is significant as the actualization by a
young architect of the concept of the garden in relation to
the house. The magic of Thomas's original garden has been
kept alive in the later additions. Athelhampton renders
itself unforgettable: with variety within enclosures bursting
with delight and detail, the playfulness and human scale of
its structure, its obvious capacity as a receptacle for happy
memories and its dreamlike timelessness.

Marcelle Hoff

Munstead Wood

Munstead Wood was the home, workplace and sanctuary of garden designer, plantswoman and writer Gertrude Jekyll (1843–1932), from 1897 until she died. The garden became legend in her lifetime, a living example of ideas shared with visitors, through her books and articles and her numerous commissions. Jekyll asked a young Edwin Lutyens (1869–1944) to design her house, the start of an internationally recognized partnership with a radical conceptual approach to garden design.

Jekyll began her garden before the house was conceived. In *Gardens for Small Country Houses* (1912), she describes the plot as 'Fifteen acres of the poorest soil, sloping a little down towards the north, in the Surrey Hills. A thin skin of peaty earth on the upper part, with a natural growth of heath, whortleberry and bracken, where a wood of Scotch fir had been cut some twelve years before; the middle part a chestnut plantation, the lower, a poor, sandy field with a hard plough-bed about eight inches down.' 'These were the conditions', she wrote, 'that had to be considered and adapted as well as might be to making a garden.'

Unlike her commissioned work, Jekyll did not have a definite plan but worked with each part on its merits, subsequently reconciling the whole. An enduring essence, the woodland garden evolved through an appreciation of the natural placing of different trees, skilfully enhanced by thinning and selected additions. A clearing became the south lawn and location of the house, the hub for all paths including the wide green walk, '... the most precious possession of the place, the bluish distance giving a sense

**Munstead Wood,
Surrey**
-
Gertrude Jekyll
-
1897–1932
-
Registered Grade I

OPPOSITE The south front of the house viewed through the woods.

BELOW Irises in the garden at Munstead Wood.

of some extent and the bounding woodland one of repose and security.' Horticultural expertise enabled her schemes of native flora and ornamental additions, especially azaleas, enhancing the woodland edges with colour and shape. Close by, a sunken rock garden augments the intrigue and a topiary cat, the charm – a nod to Jekyll's much-loved companions.

Largely intact, the north-facing paved court is a circular, calm composition using local materials in a raised pavement, pots, a garland of *Clematis montana*, stone steps and a tank, nestled among ferns, its waterspout, 'a finely designed lion mask' – signature features of future commissions.

LEFT The Long Border in summer.

OPPOSITE A stone archway in the garden.

The Nut Walk and pergola led visitors to a sunny lawn where the main flower border, 55 metres (180 feet) long and 5.5 metres (18 feet) deep, displayed Jekyll's experimental, widely admired colour-themed planting. Complex and intricate, the plan is detailed in her *Colour Schemes for the Flower Garden* (1911). Contemporary autochrome photographs illustrate these ideas, as well as Jekyll's seasonal spaces, all inventive compositions in colour, form and plant breeding, sitting alongside her working nursery and kitchen garden. In the spring garden, thin streams of colourful tulips were woven through aubretia and drifts of wallflowers. The early summer borders were a plethora of pastel iris and lupins, the September borders a pleasing tapestry of predominately Michaelmas daisies and the Grey Garden an artwork in cool and welcoming hues.

Divided and simplified in the 1950s, the garden has been restored and recreated over the last 30 years, and is now owned by the National Trust.

Sarah Dickinson

GARDENS IN THE 20TH CENTURY

———

The 20th century was a time of great ferment in British horticulture. Two world wars, de-colonization, globalization and mass immigration introduced many new influences and approaches, and while it would be impossible to corral them into strict stylistic categories, four loosely defined and overlapping groups can be discerned. The first, and most enduring, is the Arts and Crafts Movement. Reacting against the industrialization and urbanization of the late 19th century, it valued simplicity and utility, drawing inspiration from rural culture, folk art and traditional craftsmanship. Unlike the Victorian garden with its large spaces, stiff planting, jarring colours and exotic foliage, Arts and Crafts gardens evoke the intimate scale, garden rooms, indigenous plants and pastel colours of the Tudor era, an earlier, more confident age when England was flourishing.

The Arts and Crafts Movement emerged in a time of great turmoil. The Industrial Revolution had promised prosperity and opportunity, but two decades of bad weather from the 1870s had led to a succession of poor harvests; foreign imports then undercut home-grown produce, pushing down the value of agricultural land. This, plus the imposition of inheritance tax in 1894, forced many landowners to sell their estates or break them into smaller units. Often these were purchased by urban retirees, weekenders and commuters who romanticized the rural lifestyle, a romance which they expressed in Arts and Crafts-style gardens.

A key force in the popularization of gardening in the early 20th century was the glossy new lifestyle magazines such as *Country Life*, which itself was financed largely by property advertising, since its founding, in 1897, coincided with the break-up of the large estates. The editors of the glossy weekly understood the central role of rural life in the British psyche, especially that of its urban subscribers; then, as now, most of its readers were city-dwellers. For those who couldn't afford a rural estate, *Country Life* provided voyeuristic insight into what they were missing. For those who could, it acted as manual of design, showing appropriate garden layout, planting and activities.

LEFT Women in London Digging for Victory during the Second World War.

OPPOSITE Upton Grey epitomizes the popular Arts and Crafts style that remains a favourite to this day.

One of the designers who appeared frequently in the early days of *Country Life* was Gertrude Jekyll. Jekyll tended to work on sizable suburban plots or modest rural estates, which were large enough to incorporate such features of the grand country house as orchards, water gardens, vegetable, herb and rose gardens, croquet lawns and herbaceous borders. With their stone walls and terraces, wooden pergolas and rustic summerhouses, her gardens embodied Arts and Crafts ideals of tradition, craftsmanship, vernacular motifs and local materials. These tended to be superimposed on an Italianate framework of casual formality. A more modest version of this style was the cottage garden; a romantic fantasy allegedly derived from the subsistence gardens of the industrious poor, the cottage garden combined food and flowers, practicality and leisure.

Despite its roots in nostalgia, the Arts and Crafts garden was, in many ways, revolutionary; it saw the garden as a multifunctional space for the cultivation of produce as well as pleasure. It rejected bourgeois ornament and foreign exotica; it celebrated the lifestyle of the rural poor and it challenged class distinctions by promoting the idea that gardens were for everyone, not simply the rich.

Another important feature of early 20th century horticulture was the Garden City Movement. Pioneered by a failed farmer, Ebenezer Howard, it envisioned a lifestyle that provided the conveniences of city life – decent wages, entertainment and social life, with the fresh air and healthy activities of the countryside. Howard's 1902 *Garden Cities of Tomorrow*, proposed a network of towns managed by the inhabitants, with separate residential, commercial and industrial zones, all surrounded by farmland. His ideas inspired such new towns as Letchworth, Stevenage and Milton Keynes, and also informed the suburban council estates, created after the First World War to replace inner-city slums. These generally consisted of small houses with rear gardens. Designed to encourage health and self-sufficiency, these plots were large enough to accommodate an apple tree, washing line, outhouse, coal shed and vegetable garden. As late as 1935, J.B. Priestley in *The Beauty of Britain* claimed that all Englishmen are, at heart, country gentlemen, adding, 'the suburban villa enables the salesman or the clerk, out of hours, to be almost a country gentleman.'

While England's working classes were emulating country gentlemen, in Europe a new movement was brewing known as Modernism. Like the Arts and Crafts movement, Modernism was a response to industrialization, but Modernists saw technology as a solution to the problems of urban life. While they too valued simplicity and deplored Victorian ornament, rather than turn to traditional crafts, they embraced mass production. Given the bloodbath of the Great War, they condemned nationalism and vernacular styles as divisive, seeking instead an international style. Modernist garden designers experimented with new materials such as concrete, steel and glass, which were cheap, versatile and universally available. They adopted new motifs such as the grid with its suggestion of the drafting board, or the diagonal which pushed the boundaries of the space, or the dramatic zig-zag, popular in the Vorticist paintings of the time.

Pioneered largely by architects seeking a suitable setting for their modern houses, the Modernist garden tended to be formal and evergreen with spaces defined by the lines of the house. In 1938 a new, softer approach was promoted by Christopher Tunnard in *Gardens in the Modern Landscape*. Tunnard asserted that gardens should be efficient, low-maintenance and functional, providing such amenities as recreation areas, sports facilities and dining terraces. He also advocated an oriental aesthetic, based on balance and harmony rather than symmetry, and advised designers to seek inspiration in contemporary art.

By the late 1930s England was facing economic decline; this, plus the build-up of hostilities in Europe, created a resentment of foreign ideas. Britain's mercantile and colonial past had introduced many new plants that could thrive in the country's moderate climate and England's gardeners were reluctant to give up such variety for the austerities of Modernism. The Modernist style was also antithetical to commercial interests, as garden magazines, television programmes and garden centres pushed seasonal flowers rather than evergreen shrubs, to ensure a continuing market for their wares. The invention of colour film in the 1950s further favoured colourful flowers over dull evergreens, and helped undermine the Modernist approach in horticulture.

However, in the 1960s, Modernism experienced a brief revival, especially in institutional sites such as city parks or factory grounds. The garden round St Catherine's College, Oxford, designed in 1962 by the architect Arne Jacobsen, is a prime example of Modernist design with its gridded layout, strong lines drawn from the surrounding buildings and austere planting of trees and shrubs. At about the same time John Brookes adopted Modernism's functional approach, presenting the garden as an outdoor living space rather than a display ground for plants. Over the succeeding decades however, Brookes evolved from a strictly orthogonal layout, to embrace a more organic style. In gardens such as Denmans in West Sussex, the design school he established in the 1980s, Brookes created vibrant, organic spaces, which flow freely round the site, featuring amorphous beds and mass plantings to create bold blocks of colour.

Meanwhile, most British gardeners retreated to a new romantic style, also known as Neo-Arts and Crafts. The wartime Dig for Victory campaign, which had expropriated every bit of empty ground for food cultivation, engendered a post-war aversion to utilitarian landscapes and many people turned, with relief, from the labour of growing food to the pleasure of growing flowers.

This floriferous approach was exemplified by Margery Fish, who in late middle age and with no horticultural knowledge, pioneered a relaxed style of gardening around East Lambrook Manor in Somerset. More fluid than the traditional Arts and Crafts garden, less boundaried than the cottage garden, Fish's approach was loose and informal, featuring rockeries, streams, winding paths and mixed borders filled with bulbs, wild flowers, shrubs, herbs, annuals and perennials, all flowing freely through her 0.8-hectare (2-acre) site. Faced with post-war labour shortages and costs, Fish taught herself to lay paths, build dry-stone walls and propagate plants, then popularized her DIY approach through lectures, broadcasts and articles in the new magazines such as *Popular Gardening*, which sprang up to cater to a new generation of amateur gardeners.

Vita Sackville-West, creator of the much-loved Sissinghurst, promoted a similarly casual approach in her

ABOVE Arne Jacobsen's garden at St Catherine's College, Oxford, anchors the building into its landscape.

BELOW The garden at Sissinghurst was designed by Vita Sackville-West and her husband Harold Nicolson.

weekly *Observer* columns from 1946 until 1961. Here she shared ideas for new projects, described her discoveries and confessed her failures, creating an emotional link with her readers, which partly explains the extraordinary devotion that Sissinghurst inspired. Although it is routinely hailed as the classic English garden, Sissinghurst is more opulent and cosmopolitan than most domestic gardens of the time; its layout is neither symmetrical nor even predictable, and its features reveal Greek, Italian and Persian influences, garnered during Sackville-West's international travels.

Hidcote, which is also often hailed as the archetypal English garden, was created by an American who was certainly neither casual nor amateur. Lawrence Johnston had studied both architecture and agriculture and employed professional gardeners rather than doing the work himself. Though Hidcote features the conventional Arts and Crafts sequence of garden rooms, its spaces are filled with exotic plants, rare trees, crisp topiary, water features and architectural elements, while the garden itself is bigger, bolder and more extravagant than any true Arts and Crafts garden.

The continuing lure of the Arts and Crafts style, however, is evident throughout the century in such modest, suburban gardens as the 0.4-hectare (1-acre) York Gate in Leeds. Begun in 1951, it features such classic elements as paths and pavilions, interlinked vistas and garden rooms. An Arts and Crafts soul is equally evident in the 5-hectare (12-acre) garden round Saling Hall in Essex, with its walled garden, long walk, yew hedges and pleached limes. One Arts and Craft garden that has been dragged into the modern world is Great Dixter in East Sussex. Created in 1912 with typical long border, sunken garden, orchard and wildflower meadow, it was taken over in the 1950s by Christopher Lloyd, the son of the house. While 'Christo' retained the formal structures and exuberant planting, he also experimented with texture, form and colour, creating dramatic, sometimes startling and often controversial plant combinations, which make Dixter such an inspiration to contemporary garden makers.

By the late 1960s, Britain's population was finally becoming aware of ecological issues. One of the first horticulturists to take these concerns seriously was plantswoman Beth Chatto, who, through her commercial nursery and attendant gardens, promoted environmentally friendly gardening. Tackling difficult conditions such as shade and damp, she set out to position 'the right plant in the right place' – which became the mantra of a whole generation of gardeners drawn to her low-maintenance, self-sustaining approach. Chatto's Gravel Garden, created on an Essex car park in one of the driest regions in the country, has famously never been watered yet it maintains a spectacular array of flowers throughout much of the year.

The latter years of the 20th century were a time of innovation as individuals came to the fore. Often turning to gardens from other media, they forged unique and distinct gardens in a movement that has come to be known as conceptual gardening, since the designs were inspired more by an idea or a theme than a particular style.

LEFT Christopher Tunnard's minimal, functional, low-maintenance approach at Bentley Wood, East Sussex, marked a new naturalism in Modernist design.

OPPOSITE At Prospect Cottage in Kent Derek Jarman re-established horticulture as an avant-garde art form.

One of the most influential of these was Prospect Cottage, a garden wrested from the windswept shingle of the Kentish coast by avant-garde artist and *enfant terrible* Derek Jarman. Ornamenting his plot with flotsam and jetsam washed up on the beach, Jarman set himself the task of using only local flora as plant material. Some attribute the unexpectedly large range of plants he discovered to a microclimate created by hot water expelled from the Sizewell nuclear power station, which looms sublimely over the site. When Jarman was diagnosed with HIV his garden became an image of hope and defiance. By the time he died, in 1994, Prospect Cottage had established horticulture as an avant-garde art form.

Meanwhile, in the Scottish Lowlands the poet, Ian Hamilton Finlay, created an equally provocative garden in Little Sparta. More metaphorical than horticultural, it is full of sculptures and follies, gnomic inscriptions and visual puns, many of them barbed comments celebrating classical culture or deploring the superficiality of the modern world. As its creator explained: 'Gardens may look like retreats, but sometimes they are attacks.'

Also in Scotland, though created by an American architectural historian, Charles Jencks, the Garden of Cosmic Speculation took its inspiration from science rather than politics or philosophy. Fascinated by the study of cosmogenesis, Jencks attempted to find horticultural metaphors to illustrate contemporary theories of the origins of the universe. Incorporated into a 19th-century agricultural estate, the garden's prevailing motif is fractals; its mounds, lakes, bridges and terraces all reflect these wave-like patterns, which Jencks believed to be the building blocks of the universe.

From the surprisingly radical nostalgia of the Arts and Crafts Movement, through the functional austerity of the Modernist style; from the romantic retreat of the post-war period to the sheer inventiveness of conceptual designers, Britain's gardens through the 20th century reflected both the wider concerns of a tumultuous era, and the individual creativity of some extraordinarily inventive garden makers.

Katie Campbell

Hidcote Manor Garden

Hidcote Bartrim,
Chipping Campden,
Gloucestershire

–

Major Lawrence
Waterbury Johnston

–

1907–48

–

Registered Grade I

High in the Cotswolds lies a garden of 'remarkable originality .... A jungle of beauty', wrote Vita Sackville-West in 1949, a year after Hidcote Manor was transferred to the National Trust, the first property acquired because of the garden rather than the house. The garden had also featured in 1930s articles by Russell Page and Henry Avray Tipping, both applauding the botanical knowledge and design skill of its creator, Lawrence Johnston (1871–1958).

Johnston was born in Paris to wealthy American parents, moving with his mother (by then Mrs Gertrude Winthrop) to England, where he obtained a history degree from Cambridge University in 1897. He became a naturalized Briton to fight in the Second Boer War, the beginning of a 20-year career with the Northumberland Hussars, rising to the rank of major. When posted to South Africa in 1900, he became interested in its flora, becoming a fellow of the Royal Horticultural Society in 1904. In 1907, his mother bought Hidcote Manor, a farm of 121 hectares (300 acres), hoping her son would become a gentleman farmer. Johnston had other ideas, planning to develop a garden from the difficult, exposed site and the surrounding fields.

Johnston lived part-time at Hidcote until 1920, when he left the army, developing the garden in three phases, 1907–14, 1914–20 and 1920–30. He borrowed books on gardening from the RHS and was probably influenced by practitioners such as William Robinson, Edwin Lutyens, Gertrude Jekyll, Thomas Mawson and, in the later period, his friend Norah Lindsay. He adopted Mawson's concept of creating a series of spaces and developed his garden as

OPPOSITE The long borders at Hidcote in late summer.

interconnecting compartments, working outwards from the old garden south of the house. Clipped hedges provide the structural framework he had seen in the formal gardens of France and Italy on travels with his mother. Johnson had studied architecture and was an artist, so Hidcote has two long grassy walks, framing views across the garden and out into the land beyond, with informal, naturalistic areas, woodland and water gardens on each side.

Johnston's passion was horticulture, and in the 1920s he sponsored or undertook expeditions with plant hunters, such as Reginald Cory and E.A. Bowles, to Europe, Asia, Africa and South America, introducing many plants into cultivation, such as *Hypericum* 'Hidcote' and *Lavandula* 'Hidcote'. Wanting to expand the range of plants he could grow, in 1924 Johnston bought Serre de la Madone, a steeply terraced property in Menton on the French Riviera, where the Mediterranean climate allowed him to indulge his love of exotic plants. He then spent much of the year there, returning to Hidcote for the summer months. In 1948, he retired to Menton, paving the way for Hidcote to

go to the National Trust. Norah Lindsay destroyed many of Johnston's papers, so there were few garden records until in 2002, the discovery of a notebook and two diaries provided information on the later planting.

Johnston died at Serre de la Madone on 27 April 1958 and is buried alongside his mother (d. 1926) in Mickleton churchyard, near Hidcote.

Barbara Simms

ABOVE A sundial, euphorbias and bronze cordylines are features of Mrs Winthrop's Garden.

LEFT Clipped hornbeam trees and clean gravel paths form the Stilt Garden.

FAR LEFT One of the lush herbaceous borders at Hidcote, overflowing with summer colour.

The Japanese Garden at Cowden

In February 1907, Ella Christie (1861–1949) and her lady's maid set off on a journey by ocean-going liner, Chinese junk, bullock cart, train and river boat through South East Asia, China and Korea. They arrived in Japan in time for *hanami* or cherry blossom viewing. Miss Christie was captivated and determined to build a Japanese garden in her estate outside Dollar. The result was Sha Raku En, 'the place of pleasure and delight', a 3-hectare (7-acre) strolling garden built around a lake with traditional features, using *shakkei* (borrowed landscape) to fit in seamlessly beneath the Ochil Hills.

Miss Christie engaged Taki Handa (1871–1956), a horticulture student at Studley College, Warwickshire, to design it. Taki visited three times, to plan the garden and oversee the estate workers. By the time she returned to Japan in 1908, only the lanterns from Japan needed to be installed. Around 1925 Miss Christie engaged Professor Jiju Suzuki, a Japanese garden designer based in London, to prune the plants and make improvements, notably replacing a curved bridge to the island with a zig-zag *yatsuhashi* bridge. He also found a Japanese gardener, Shinzaburo Matsuo, who worked at Cowden from 1927–35.

When Miss Christie died in 1949, Cowden was inherited by her great nephew, Sir Robert Stewart. In 1963 the garden was vandalized, the lanterns pushed into the lake, the tea house burned down, and the remains disappeared beneath the encroaching rhododendrons. In the 1990s the Garden History Society in Scotland was an advocate for the restoration of the garden, seeing that the bones of it were still there. From 2014, Sara Stewart began a faithful

Dollar,
Clackmannanshire

-

Taki Handa

-

1908

OPPOSITE The view towards the Upper Entrance Gate on Mount Fuji.

BELOW The original garden c. 1909.

LEFT View of the *karesansui* (dry garden) and *azumaya* (summer pavilion).

ABOVE The Upper Entrance Gate and the Drum Bridge.

restoration, with the help of Professor Masao Fukuhara of Osaka University of Arts.

Unlike other Western Japanese gardens, Cowden was created and maintained by Japanese people, providing an authentic experience. There is a *karesansui* or dry garden where an arrangement of four moss-covered islands floats in a sea of raked gravel, the *azumaya* in the background, overlooking the lake, from which the garden can be enjoyed in all weathers. The soils of Japan and Scotland are similar, so Taki Handa could use many plants typically found in Japan, though she used some local plants to give a fusion of Scottish and Japanese culture. The paths meander through azaleas, irises, maples, pines, hydrangeas and ferns, all of which thrive here, as does moss in the damp climate. Moss is an important element in Japanese gardens, particularly some which Miss Christie would have seen in Kyoto. She was an enthusiastic collector of seeds; some of the larger trees have grown from seeds that she brought back, others from seeds collected in California by Sir Robert Stewart.

The garden is now maintained by two gardeners and local volunteers, and restoration continues. It is managed by a charitable trust, Cowden Castle SCIO, and is open all year, as any true Japanese garden is not dependent only on the planting, but also the structure that enables one to see the beauty and spirit whatever the season.

Lucy Stewart

Allerton Cemetery

Woolton Road,
Liverpool

-

John C. Brodie

-

Opened 1909

-

Registered Grade II

Liverpool was a city of major importance in the development of the modern cemetery. Two of the pioneering examples of the 1820s were constructed in Liverpool: the Liverpool Necropolis or Low Hill Cemetery (1825), for Dissenters, and St James's Cemetery (1829) for Anglicans. But a growing city needs to have its burial facilities extended periodically, and as Liverpool's population grew from 120,000 in the 1820s to nearly 700,000 at the turn of the century, the great cemeteries of Toxteth Park (1856) and Anfield (1863) – the architect T.D. Barry working respectively with William Gay and Edward Kemp, the most important cemetery designers of the time – were added, along with four other municipal cemeteries and two Roman Catholic ones. And still the pressure for burial space mounted. In 1898, the Necropolis, having reached its capacity, was closed and re-landscaped as Grant Gardens.

At the beginning of the 20th century, Liverpool planned a cemetery that would be the best 'not only of the empire but of the world'. The Burials Committee was sent on a tour of European cemeteries in order to find the best examples to follow, and came back particularly taken with the new forest cemeteries of Berlin. The design of the new cemetery at Allerton was entrusted to the City Engineer John A. Brodie (1858-1934), who was later to become known for his promotion of dual carriageways and prefabricated housing. Allerton Cemetery was opened in 1909.

The entrance gates are approached by a long straight road, which originally crossed a large area devoted to allotments, that was later added to the cemetery. The view

OPPOSITE Part of Allerton's tree cover, opening into glades and areas laid out to grass.

from the gates originally revealed an expanse of formal lawn on either side of the road (an effect somewhat reduced today by a trickle of prominent graves being added). Once past the gates, this main road gently veers away from a straight course, and in the grounds on either side it is flanked by major curving roads, after which it briefly divides into a roundabout within which stands the Anglican chapel. Dissenters' and Roman Catholic chapels are sited off this main axis. All three chapels were designed by Brodie. Along the way hedges and clumps of trees serve to close off views and divide the cemetery visually into different sectors, to reduce the uniform effect of rows of gravestones. In keeping with Edwardian fashion, some of the tree groups were planned for the display of foliage colours.

The cemetery has been extended more than once, and the largest contemporary section is separated from the main burial ground by a woodland path, keeping the forest cemetery idea going. In 1975, Springwood Crematorium was opened across the street; most recently, an area for woodland burials has been developed.

Today, tourists visiting Allerton Cemetery are most likely in search of the graves of Cilla Black and Ken Dodd, rather than the trees. But its nearly 60 hectares (148 acres) offer not only monuments, but an important landscape which, through the writings of Leo Godseff (1876–1959), a later superintendent, influenced the development of British cemetery design.

Brent Elliott

Great Dixter

Arguably the most significant horticulturally focused garden in Britain, Great Dixter is governed by constantly evolving aesthetic decision-making and a tight maintenance regime that results in a level of connoisseurship, which it is difficult to envisage anywhere else. Under the leadership of Fergus Garrett, it has also emerged as an international leader in the training of gardeners, attracting students from all around the world, who stay for up to a year.

The Dixter approach is one of minutely observed aesthetic considerations, and related daily decision-making, coupled with an emphasis on horticultural innovation – and occasional iconoclasm. This was established under the acutely watchful eye of Christopher Lloyd, who was born and brought up at Dixter, and took over management of the garden at his mother's death in 1972. Renowned as a writer and connoisseur of plants, Lloyd remained in charge until his death in 2006, with Garrett joining him as head gardener in 1993, latterly as his creative horticultural partner.

It was in 1910 that Christopher's father, Nathaniel Lloyd, bought the broken-down farmhouse, dating from about 1460. Edwin Lutyens was engaged to help with the renovation of house and garden, and it was he who decided to retain the barns and outbuildings in their original positions, which helps to give the garden its unique personality and sense of permanence. A medieval hall house, due to be demolished 14.5 kilometres (9 miles) away, was moved brick by brick to Dixter to form a new wing.

The new garden was defined by a simple system of yew-hedged enclosures made on the sloping terrain above the

East Sussex
–
**Nathaniel Lloyd;
Christopher Lloyd;
Fergus Garrett**
–
1910
–
Registered Grade I

OPPOSITE The long border eschews the precepts of Arts and Crafts colour theory in favour of challenging combinations.

LEFT The house provides stability at the centre of a constantly changing horticultural extravaganza.

house, which is sited near the top edge of the Rother Valley. This creates a sense that the garden is hugging the house, almost as if to stop itself from tumbling into the valley, with the long border anchoring it laterally. Meanwhile, the slope below is left relatively unadorned, as meadow grass and orchard, creating an intimate and then open dynamic.

What feels like the principal area of the garden can be found on the rising ground to the east, in the hedged enclosures. These contain a diversity of perennial plants, choice annuals and a few defining shrubs, envisaged as a series of continually changing pictures which grow and meld into each other. These complex episodes are carefully planned — in Lloyd's time with an emphasis on vivid, uncompromising colour contrasts, while under Garrett more linking plants create a sense of continuity. The iconoclasm is perhaps most apparent in the exuberantly colourful Exotic Garden below the house, formerly the rose garden, where large-leaved cannas and bananas vie with red *Dahlia* 'Bishop of Llandaff' and purple *Verbena bonariensis* – signature plants here, and a look much emulated elsewhere. The long border at Dixter is justly celebrated, planned as a never-ending succession of highlights. But this garden is unusual in that all of its parts are subject to the same close scrutiny.

Great Dixter operates at a different level to most gardens. As Lloyd once commented: 'This is not a fluffy cottage garden that just continues smoothly on. It is a place where we have always been expressive.'

Tim Richardson

Wicksteed Park

Kettering,
Northamptonshire

–

Charles Wicksteed

–

Opened 1921

–

Registered Grade II

Many historic parks and gardens were created for family recreation, yet today, garden visiting often feels like a genteel pursuit for sensible, grown-up people. Not at Wicksteed Park.

This uniquely playful park was created within an 18th-century parkland landscape that had been worked on by Humphry Repton. Engineer Charles Wicksteed bought the land in 1913 to build social housing, but changed direction to make a public park. Charles was passionate about the value of access to outdoor space and the importance of play: 'It is as natural for a child to run about, to jump and play, as it is for a dog – it is their joy of life .... It encourages healthy tastes, good temper and a healthy body; can anybody deny this?' The park Charles made boasts plenty of space for jumping and playing, as well as a boating lake, 1920s tea pavilion, model railway, rose garden for 'tired mothers', and a Grade II-listed, early 20th-century water chute ride – what more could visitors possibly want?

The answer is, children's playground equipment! At the time of the First World War, when Charles first opened the park, children's playgrounds were by no means the norm, so he didn't provide one until 'We had a Sunday School Treat in the Park and put up primitive swings with larch poles, tied together at the top with chains. Fortunately they were not cleared away with the other things the day after the treat, and I ultimately found them so popular that instead of pulling them down I added more to them. But these were not enough for the children, I found them piling up forms one above another on a slope under a tree to form

OPPOSITE The lake at Wicksteed Park was created by Charles Wicksteed and opened in 1921.

a slide, and breaking them. As a consequence I thought I would make a slide: first for the boys. This was so much appreciated that I made a better one for the girls: the boys got jealous of this, so I made a still better one for them.'

Charles went on to build more and more play equipment, and over time grew his engineering business so that it became a world-wide sector leader, setting global expectations for playgrounds in every park. The Wicksteed Park playground was used as a showroom of sorts, with a dizzying array of kit: plane swings, plank swings, see-saw swings; rowing see-saws, see-saw ladders and non-bumper see-saws; giant-strides, ocean waves, merry-go-rounds, joy wheels, whirling platforms, slides, trapeze rings, horizontal bars, horizontal ladders, parallel bars, leapfrog bucks, jungle gyms and rocking horses.

Today, Wicksteed Park is flourishing thanks to several invaluable National Lottery grants, first to restore the lake, and then the 1920s heart of the park with pavilion, bungalows and kiosks. The playground continues to buzz with children, and now includes playable replicas of historic features such as wooden slides, a witch's hat and a Jungle Gym climbing frame.

Wicksteed Park is in the unusual and challenging position of being a free public park but without local authority funding, instead being cared for by the Wicksteed Charitable Trust. The park recently celebrated its centenary – may it flourish for another hundred years.

Linden Groves

The map labels, reading across the illustration, include:

Water Chute · Children's Drying Rooms · Toilets · Pets Corner · Tunnel · Clubhouse Kettering Rowing Club · Miniature Car Track · Aviaries · Children's Boating · Boating · Motor Launch · The Lake · Paxton's Bridge · Cold Drinks Ice Cream · Miniature Railway Station · Children's Paddling Pool · Children's Bathing Pool · Model Yacht Pond · Water Filter House · Shelter · Cycle Track · Memorial to 'Jerry' the dog constant companion of Mr Charles Wicksteed · Sunken Gardens Bandstand · Sports Arena · Sweets Ice Cream Fruit · CAR PARK · RESTAURANT · Toilets · CAR PARK · WAY OUT · 18 HOLE Golf Course · ENTRANCE · COACH PARK · Ice Cream & Sweets · Ice Cream · Picnic Counters · ICE CREAM SERVERY · Toy Shop · Shelter & Amusement Hall · Mini Jet Ride · Pony Riding · NO PARKING · NO THROUGH ROAD · A.A. R.A.C. & POLICE · Joywheel · Roundabout · FIRST AID STATION LOST CHILDREN & PROPERTY · Cloakrooms Toilets · Ice Cream Factory · ENTRANCE · Children's Playground · Sand Pit · Coaster · Central Ticket Office · Helter Skelter · Mini Dodgems · Putting Green · Tennis Courts · MAIN OFFICES · THE WICKSTEED PARK KETTERING · TO WELLINGBOROUGH · A6 TO BEDFORD · ENTRANCE · BUS STOP · TO KETTERING · BUS STOP

ABOVE A map of Wicksteed Park, packed with entertainment.

OPPOSITE ABOVE In 2015, a sculpture was commissioned to represent Hilda Wicksteed as a child in the 1920s, together with a modern child, Victor.

OPPOSITE BELOW Wicksteed branding is famous on play equipment across the world.

East Lambrook Manor

In 1980, John Sales, then Head of Gardens for the National Trust said of East Lambrook Manor, in Somerset, that 'in the development of gardening in the second half of the twentieth century, no garden has yet had greater effect.' This effect was to create a passion in Britain for the 'cottage garden' style of planting brought to prominence through the enthusiasm and hard work of its creator, Margery Fish (1892–1969).

Walter and Margery Fish bought East Lambrook Manor (Grade II*) in 1938. Until his death in 1949, the pair developed the garden together but often warred over differences in styles. Walter insisted on rolled gravel paths and neatly edged lawns, and was keen on showy delphiniums, dahlias and hybrid tea roses. Margery, on the other hand, wanted to keep self-sown seedlings and reputedly, unbeknown to Walter, toured the garden surreptitiously sprinkling seeds from holes in her pockets.

The terrain of the garden, almost 0.8 hectares (2 acres) in size, included small areas of sun and shade but also a marsh by a ditch and an orchard, none of which suited the long, wide herbaceous borders popular at the time. Mrs Fish changed the lie of the land, excavating barrowfuls of heavy clay subsoil and building dry stone retaining walls herself. Areas include the Silver Garden and the Stone Terrace, while others are more prosaically known as the Strip, the Ditch and the Lido. The Barton was a farmyard area until planted by her in the 1940s.

Fish was keen to have flowers blooming all year round, the subject of a later book. All her books, starting with *We Made a Garden* published in 1956, show her in-depth

East Lambrook,
Somerset
–
Margery Fish MBE
–
1938–69
–
Registered Grade I

OPPOSITE A narrow winding path is almost hidden by the packed cottage-style planting.

BELOW The relaxed planting complements the warm honey tones of the Somerset stone manor house.

OPPOSITE The Ditch belies its name with carpets of snowdrops as winter ends.

RIGHT Self-seeders such as *Smyrnium perfoliatum* and *Anthriscus sylvestris* are welcomed to fill spring borders.

knowledge of plant material. It was estimated after she died that she had amassed over 2,000 different species, varieties and cultivars. Her interest fell into two categories. First, herbaceous plants such as hellebores, sedums and hardy geraniums, all of which she pioneered for year-round interest without the need for elaborate staking and maintenance. Many were discovered by her or given to her to propagate by friends such as Lawrence Johnston of Hidcote Manor, Nancy Lindsay and a close neighbour, Violet Clive of Brympton d'Evercy.

After Walter's death, Mrs Fish indulged in her passions for hellebores, snowdrops, primroses and epimediums among others. By 1960, her nursery listed 11 campanulas, 13 euphorbias, 15 decorative grasses but nearly 60 cultivars of primroses. It continues to offer a selection of rare plants from the garden.

Margery Fish's aim was always to promote what she felt was a disappearing heritage of the true English cottage-garden style – colourful and long-lasting but also unmanicured and low maintenance. Long after her death in 1969, her books remain invaluable for those who have fallen for this relaxed way of planting. The garden has since passed through three different owners' hands, all of whom worked extremely hard to preserve its Grade-I legacy and it continues to attract visitors keen to enjoy this showcase of a traditional garden style.

Catherine Horwood

Denmans Garden

OPPOSITE The garden is a series of spaces that flow one into another elegantly but informally.

BELOW Joyce Robinson's gravel gardens were inspired by visits to the Greek island of Delos.

Fontwell, West Sussex

–

Joyce Robinson and John Brookes MBE

–

1947–85

–

Registered Grade II

Denmans was initially created by self-taught plantswoman Joyce Robinson (1903–96) and later developed by landscape designer John Brookes (1933–2018). It pioneered abundant, naturalistic planting and gravel gardening, which became influential through the work of Brookes as a designer, teacher and writer.

In 1946, the Robinsons bought the requisitioned estate, and started renovating the dilapidated gardens and gardener's cottage to create a productive market garden. Mrs Robinson soon began ornamental gardening, incorporating some plants, such as *Parrotia persica* and *Stachyurus praecox*, from their previous home. She never worked professionally, but became a knowledgeable plantswoman by visiting local nurseries, botanical gardens and RHS shows, and wrote articles for the *West Sussex Gazette*.

Mrs Robinson described her planting style as 'glorious disarray'. She created her first gravel garden in 1970 in the walled garden, to the east of the cottage. Convinced that she could recreate the natural landscape of rampant plants and stonework she loved on the Greek island of Delos, she laid local gravel and allowed plants to self-sow and ramble, nurturing only those she wanted.

In 1977 she created two new gravel 'stream' beds in a redundant calf paddock, using gravel, sandstone and ironstone rocks. The illusion of a stream was enhanced by low banks of earth around the dry river hole at the end of the beds and a large, water-worn stepping stone. The beds were planted with grasses, bulbs, irises, thistles, mint, willow, elder and drifts of violets. She extended her garden

to the south, later adding a circular pond which Brookes integrated into the gravel garden that swept across to the Victorian conservatory. To the south-east a lawn was laid and left to grow long during the summer, creating different textures and encouraging flowering.

John Brookes discovered Denmans through the Open Gardens scheme, and in 1979, after working in Tehran and India, he approached Mrs Robinson about moving to Denmans. He went on to garden there for the next 38 years, testing ideas for potential in his design work, free from clients' requirements. He set up his Clock House School of Design in the stable block in 1980.

Brookes spent the rest of his life revising the beds and walks, creating garden rooms that embraced Mrs. Robinson's gravel gardens. He introduced his iconic blue timber benches, additional native and exotic plants and created curved beds and shapes throughout the garden,

influenced by artist and ecologist Roberto Burle Marx. He later referred to his approach of combining planting with strong architectural and structural elements as one of 'controlled disarray'. The garden north of the Clock House was remodelled to a design influenced by artist Piet Mondrian, as his *Room Outside*, the title of his seminal garden design book (1969).

After a partnership with businessman Michael Neve failed, putting the garden at risk, it was rescued in 2017 with assistance from Peter Gillespie and Gwendolyn van Paasschen; the latter subsequently began restoring the gardens with Mr Brookes. Denmans was listed in August 2020 as part of the Garden Trust's campaign to protect significant post-war landscapes.

Virginia Hinze

FAR LEFT The garden has year-round interest, structure and colour.

ABOVE The circular pond was added in 1982.

RIGHT The climate, soil and position at Denmans make it ideal for growing a large range of plants, including species from the Mediterranean and other warmer regions.

Beth Chatto Gardens

Often claimed by its creator to have less rainfall than Egypt, the Beth Chatto Gardens are renowned for the Gravel Garden, which hasn't been watered other than by rain since it was planted in 1991. Yet this is only one small part of a palette of gardens designed for different conditions by world-famous plantswoman Beth Chatto (1923–2018). Across the 2.8-hectare (7-acre) site in Elmstead Market, east of Colchester in Essex, she created first the damp or water garden with its spring-fed stream, then the woodland garden, a scree garden for sun-loving alpines, and the Reservoir Garden, all following her principles of growing the right plant in the right place.

Beth and Andrew Chatto moved to Elmstead Market in 1960 with a van full of plants and encouragement from their plantsman friend Cedric Morris. The land, which had previously been part of Andrew's fruit farm, encircles the split-level home they commissioned for the family. While Andrew Chatto began a life-long study of plant ecology, Beth began realizing her dream of creating a group of unique garden areas. With more interest in shape and form than colour, the gardens are rare in offering something of interest throughout the year.

Beth started a career as a flower arranging demonstrator and grew her own plant material. In 1967, such was the demand for these plants, many given to her as seeds or cuttings by Cedric Morris and other horticultural friends, she opened the Unusual Plants nursery on a site close to the house. A stellar career followed, with exhibits at RHS shows and ten gold medals at Chelsea during the 1970s and

Elmstead Market,
Essex
-
Beth Chatto OBE,
VHM
-
1960–2018
-
Registered Grade II

RIGHT Drifts of *Primula bulleyana* and *Astilbe* 'Fanal' with ferns *Matteuccia struthiopteris* and *Osmunda regalis* in the Damp Garden.

LEFT Pastel puffs of *Thalictrum aquilegiifolium*.

BELOW LEFT Snowdrops carpet the Woodland Garden.

OPPOSITE Silvery wands of *Stipa barbata* emerge from *Ballota pseudodictamnus* in the Gravel Garden.

1980s. Having trained as a teacher when her first loves were English and botany, it is no surprise that her books remain popular and essential reading for keen gardeners.

At the Chelsea Flower Show, Beth had pioneered grouping displays of plants depending on their needs, and this continues in the nursery where they are divided according to their requirements. Due to the rarity of many plants grown in the gardens, the nursery continues to supply other important UK gardens and leading garden designers.

Following the Great Storm of 1987, Beth developed the Woodland Garden showcasing plants and bulbs for shady areas. Buoyed by its success, she transformed the former car park into the Gravel Garden to expand and experiment with plants for dry areas. This has led to copies across the world but few matching Beth's skill at preparation and plant placement. With increasing awareness of global climate change, she foresaw the need for gardeners to adjust horticultural practices and reduce water usage.

Her passion for education survives in the many courses and activities at the gardens through her education trust where the team continue her mission for climate awareness. As James Hitchmough, Emeritus Professor of Horticultural Ecology, confirms, 'Beth's garden was perhaps the most original British horticultural creation of the twentieth century. It will continue to have a profound effect on designers across the world in the twenty-first century.'

Catherine Horwood

Little Sparta

Biggar, Lanark
-
Ian Hamilton Finlay
-
1966

It was in 1966 that Ian Hamilton Finlay (1925–2006) and his wife Sue moved to the isolated farmstead of Stonypath, at the southern end of the Pentland Hills, to the south of Edinburgh. Finlay was already a well-known if somewhat contentious figure in the art world when they began to transform this bleak and unpromising site into a garden that is now widely recognized as being of international significance.

From early beginnings in the 1950s, Finlay had made his reputation as a concrete poet long before he began work on the property, which he rechristened Little Sparta as a counterbalance to Edinburgh's reputation as the Athens of the North. The formation of the garden began with the diversion of the Anston Burn to create a series of ponds around which the garden continued to evolve over some 40 years. By the time of his Finlay's death in 2006, the garden had become an open-air gallery containing nearly 300 artworks in a variety of materials, many of them developed in collaboration with other artists and craftspeople. It is possible to identify recurring themes in these artworks reflecting Finlay's particular interest in classical writers and figures, in the French Revolution, in the Second World War, and in ships and the sea. Also evident is Finlay's fascination with the meaning of words, often expressed in a humorous way.

There are several distinct elements within the garden – the Front Garden overlooked by the house, incorporating the Roman Garden and Allotment; Julie's Garden sheltered by trees; the Temple Pool Garden at the rear of the house replacing the former farmyard; the adjoining Woodland

OPPOSITE A view across Lochan Eck, named after Ian's son Alec, carries the eye across the valley of South Edwin Water to the distant heather-covered hill of Black Mount.

ABOVE LEFT The tablet inscribed with the words 'Line Light Lade', to be found in the English Parkland, is just one of many examples of Ian's love of alliteration and his play on words.

LEFT The first of a series of tablets forming the inscription, 'Folding the Last Sheep'. Fixed to three walls of a dry-stone walled enclosure named 'Eclogue', this feature is inspired by the pastoral poems of the Roman poet Virgil.

RIGHT Within the Wild Garden the gilded head of *Apollon Terroriste* reflects Finlay's interest in classical sculpture, but also alludes to the French revolutionary Louis de Saint-Just, known as the Archangel of Terror.

Garden; the Wild Garden leading up towards the moorland beyond; the Lochan Eck Garden with its wide open views; the English Parkland Garden created in the 1990s; and the intimate Hortus Conclusus in a roofless building, being the last part of the garden to have been added. Among those artworks that have achieved near-iconic status are the *Nuclear Sail*, his monument to the French Revolutionary Louis de Saint-Just, a bird table in the shape of an aircraft carrier, and his stone with the punning inscription 'See Poussin, Hear Lorrain'.

Little Sparta became celebrated in the 1980s for Finlay's confrontation with Strathclyde Regional Council over the payment of rates for one of the farm buildings. Attempts to confiscate some of the artworks in lieu of rates led to the First Battle of Little Sparta in which the visit of a Regional Council officer in 1983 was famously repulsed by Finlay's friends and supporters in the form of the so-called Saint-Just Vigilantes.

The Little Sparta Trust was formed in 2005, with the object of securing the future of the garden, along with his library and archive, and of allowing public access to what the late Charles Jencks described in 1993 as 'probably the most significant recent creative garden in Britain'. A profusely illustrated book by Jessie Sheeler is recommended for anyone interested in the inspiration behind Finlay's artworks.

Christopher Dingwall

Campbell Park

This imaginative, 45-hectare (111-acre) people's park has a landscape design loosely based on Central Park in New York. It is a key element of the planned cityscape, linking the urban centre through naturalistic parkland to the Ouse Valley. The park lies on an axis with the shopping centre to the west and rises to a mound in the east, offering exhilarating panoramic views to Willen Lake, the Newlands Tree Cathedral and Bedfordshire countryside beyond.

Designer Neil Higson said: 'Our plan was to create a unified composition of various landscape types, partly developed from existing and adjusted landform and partly guided by character and function as elements of a people's park. We were, after all, dedicated followers of Ebenezer Howard's Garden City Movement, as well as believing that landscape can have a fundamental influence on the health and quality of life of all citizens, and in consequence the success of the new city.' Originally it was intended to be an international sculpture park, although financial cuts meant that just eight significant sculptures were originally installed, but more have been added in recent years.

A network of paths cross the central grassed area, which is planted with groups of trees, and has some individual oaks that pre-date the park. The trees have been thinned to provide wonderful views across the park, evoking the landscape style of Lancelot 'Capability' Brown. Areas alongside paths are mown to give reassurance that the park is managed. Otherwise, the sward is left uncut until mid- to late summer before being cut for hay as a crop for livestock, and periodically grazed by sheep.

Milton Keynes

Neil Higson, Chief Landscape Architect, Milton Keynes Development Corporation
-
1977–84
-
Registered Grade II

LEFT The *Armillary Sphere* at the centre of the Labyrinth. Justin Tunley, 1995.

OPPOSITE Axial view of Central Milton Keynes, with Campbell Park in the foreground.

OPPOSITE The Milton Keynes Rose, a place of reflection. Gordon Young, 2013.

RIGHT The watercourse runs through the north section of the park.

BELOW RIGHT The *Light Pyramid* located at the end of the belvedere. Liliane Lijn, 2012.

At the highest point of the park, on the mound or Belvedere, is the *Light Pyramid*, commissioned from Liliane Lijn in 2012 to replace a basket beacon, which had been hit by lightning in 2002. The *Light Pyramid* was first lit to celebrate Queen Elizabeth II's Diamond Jubilee in 2012 and is used to commemorate special local and national events.

The Milton Keynes Rose is a public space designed for commemoration, celebration and contemplation. Developed in partnership with the Cenotaph Trust, and designed by artist Gordon Young in 2014, it is an open-air circle with markings based on the mathematical beauty of a flower. The artwork consists of 106 granite pillars of varying height, 66 of which have been engraved with dedications, including significant dates in the history of Milton Keynes, leaving 40 for future inscriptions.

North of the Rose is the Labyrinth, which has a functional sundial, *Armillary Sphere* by Justin Tunley (1995). This is a turf maze with stone setts in the grass, and is surrounded by evergreen shrubs to give wind protection. This area, as well as that along the Belvedere, used to have specially designed seats, with canopies made of metal and glass, but these have recently been removed.

Since 1992 Campbell Park has been the responsibility of the Milton Keynes Parks Trust alongside all the other parks and green spaces in the city. Today, it continues to be developed in a similar character and is maintained to a high standard.

Claire de Carle

Plaz Metaxu

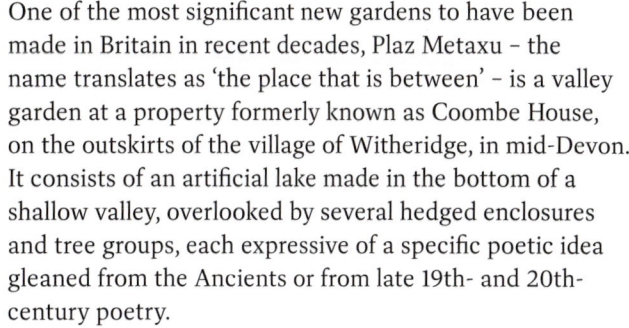

Witheridge, Devon
–
Alasdair Forbes
–
1992

OPPOSITE View north west across the valley and garden from the Dragon's Teeth in Eos.

BELOW The larger courtyard (Hermes) showing part of the Labyrinth of the Broken Heart.

One of the most significant new gardens to have been made in Britain in recent decades, Plaz Metaxu – the name translates as 'the place that is between' – is a valley garden at a property formerly known as Coombe House, on the outskirts of the village of Witheridge, in mid-Devon. It consists of an artificial lake made in the bottom of a shallow valley, overlooked by several hedged enclosures and tree groups, each expressive of a specific poetic idea gleaned from the Ancients or from late 19th- and 20th-century poetry.

As Forbes has said: 'A garden is inseparable from its legends. It needs, as well as walking, reading.' In this sense the garden's impact can be bracketed with that of Ian Hamilton Finlay's garden at Little Sparta, an impression bolstered by the use throughout the garden of inscribed stones with brief quotations from sources including Virgil, Hölderlin and Georg Trakl. But this comparison quickly breaks down on examination, as Forbes's method is more allusive (and perhaps elusive) than Finlay's, being dependent on oblique references to the characteristics of deities such as Pan or Hermes, with a special emphasis on the ambiguities and contradictions they contain. Even the shape of the land itself is suggestive of such ideas, because for Forbes, a valley creates a topographical expression of a caesura — a place that is 'between'. Where Finlay was specific to the point of polemical in his exciting use of fiercely juxtaposed imagery, Forbes has created quiet yet energetic, interlinked spaces, which are allowed to 'breathe' in terms of their own potential meanings.

ABOVE A view across
the lake to Eleusis.

ABOVE RIGHT Imbros:
a pair of standing stones.

The garden stretches westwards along the valley bottom, passing several enclosures of hornbeam hedge named for places in antiquity – first Ithaka and then Imbros (dignified by megaliths) – before it divides around the long lake which spreads west–east, the southern side elaborating into a warren of shrubberies, copses and the labyrinthine Hades and Eleusis enclosures. The Hades enclosure, one of many intense pockets of meaning in the garden, is lined with upright slates (simply old roof slates) that resemble headstones. Forbes is at pains to imbue the episodes he creates with a sense of open-endedness, and has stated that specific references are only included so that they may be forgotten. So despite the depth and complexity of its meanings, this is not a garden which requires a handguide to understand it – though Forbes has produced a book about the garden, for those who wish to understand its references.

After the openness of the exposed and often windy valley garden, and the Pastoral Loop that encircles it at high level, there is a change of pace around the Regency farmhouse, where a series of immaculate cobbled courtyards – named Distress Retort – are somehow redolent of classical Japanese design, with specimen trees and simple sculptures creating tableaux. Visitors are requested not to step on to the raked gravel spaces. This is the place where, 'the garden licks its wounds and gathers its courage'. Plaz Metaxu continues to be developed.

Tim Richardson

RIGHT Sculptures within clipped hornbeam hedging surrounded by wild planting.

Index

Further Reading

General

Katie Campbell, *British Gardens in Time: The Greatest Gardens and the People who shaped them*, Frances Lincoln, 2014

Katie Campbell, *Policies and Pleasaunces: a Guide to the Gardens of Scotland*, Barn Elms Publishing, 2007

Hazel Conway & Paul Rabbitts, *People's Parks: The Design and Development of Public Parks in Britain*, John Hudson Publishing, 2023

Penny David, *Rooted in History: Celebrating Carmarthenshire's Parks & Gardens*, Fern Press, 2017

Francesca Greenoak, *The Gardens of the National Trust for Scotland*, Aurum, 2005

Clare Hickman, *The Doctor's Garden: Medicine, Science and Horticulture in Britain*, Yale, 2022

Penelope Hobhouse & Ambra Edwards, *The Story of Gardening*, 2019

Caroline Holmes, *Where the Wilderness Pleases: The English Garden Celebrated*, ACC Art Books, 2021

Stephen Lacey, *Gardens of the National Trust*, National Trust Books, 2023

Gillian Mawrey & Linden Groves, *The Gardens of English Heritage*, Frances Lincoln, 2010

Charles Quest-Ritson, *The English Garden: A Social History*, Viking, 2001

Michael Symes, *A Glossary of Garden History*, Shire, 2006

Elisabeth Whittle, *The Historic Gardens of Wales*, The Stationery Office, 1992

16th Century

Jill Francis, *Gardens and Gardening in Early Modern England and Wales*, Yale, 2018

Paula Henderson, *The Tudor House and Garden: Architecture and Landscape in the 16th and Early 17th Centuries*, Yale/Paul Mellon Centre for Studies in British Art, 2005

Anna Keay & John Watkins, *The Elizabethan Garden at Kenilworth Castle*, English Heritage, 2013

Twigs Way, *The Tudor Garden 1485-1603*, Shire Library, 2013

17th Century

Penny David, *A Garden Lost in Time: Mystery of the Ancient Gardens of Aberglasney*, Weidenfeld & Nicolson, 2000

John Evelyn, *Sylva, or a discourse of forest-trees*, London, 1664

John Evelyn, *Elysium Britannicum*, ed. John Ingram, University of Pennsylvania Press, 2001

Stephen A. Harris, *Oxford Botanic Garden & Arboretum: A Brief History*, Bodleian Library, 2017

Simon Hiscock & Chris Thorogood, *Oxford Botanic Garden: a Guide*, Bodleian Library, 2019

David Jacques, *Gardens of Court and Country: English Design 1630–1730*, Yale, 2017

David Jacques, 'Garden Design in the mid-Seventeenth Century', in *Architectural History: Festschrift for John Newman*, Vol. 44, 2001

Fiona Jamieson et al, *Drummond Castle Gardens*, 1993, reprint 2022

William Lawson, *A New Orchard and Garden*, London, 1618

George London and Henry Wise, *The compleat gard'ner*, 1699

Luke Morgan, Nature as Model: *Salomon de Caus and Early Seventeenth-Century Landscape Design*, Philadelphia, 2007

John Parkinson, *Paradisus Terrestris*, London, 1629

Clifford E. Thornton, *A History of Birkenhead Park*, Metropolitan Borough of Wirral

Stephen Wass, *Seventeenth-Century Water Gardens*, Windgather, 2022

John Worlidge, *Systema Horti-Culturae: Or The Art of Gardening*, London, 1677

18th Century

David Brown & Tom Williamson, *Lancelot Brown and the Capability Men: Landscape Revolution in Eighteenth-Century England*, Reaktion, London, 2016

Stephen Daniels, *Humphry Repton: Landscape Gardening & the Geography of Georgian England*, Yale, London, 1999

Kate Felus, *The Secret Life of the Georgian Garden: Beautiful Objects and Agreeable Retreats*, I B Tauris, London, 2016

David Jacques, *Georgian Gardens: the Reign of Nature,* Batsford, London, 1990

Sally Jeffery, 'Hawksmoor's Vision of Wray Wood, Castle Howard', *Architectural History* 61 (2018) 37–72

Jennifer Macve, *The Hafod Landscape*, Hafod Trust, 2004

Mark Newman, *The Wonder of the North: Fountains Abbey and Studley Royal*, Boydell Press, 2015

John Phibbs, *Place-making: The Art of Capability Brown*, Historic England, 2017

John Phibbs, *Humphry Repton: Designing the Landscape Garden*, Rizzoli, 2021

Tim Richardson, *The Arcadian Friends*, Transworld, 2015

Val Scully, Helen MacFarlane & Harry Beamish, *A People's History of Gibside*, Oak Books, 2021

Michael Symes, *The Picturesque and the later Georgian Garden*, Redcliffe Press, 2012

Michael Symes, *Mr Hamilton's Elysium: The Gardens of Painshill*, Frances Lincoln, 2010

Michael Symes, *The English Rococo Garden*, Shire Garden History, 2005

Tom Williamson, *Humphry Repton: Landscape Design in an Age of Revolution*, 2020

Tom Williamson, *Polite Landscapes: Gardens and Society in Eighteenth-Century England*, Suttons, 1995

19th Century

Mavis Batey, *Regency Gardens*, Shire Garden History, 1995

Richard Bisgrove, *William Robinson: The Wild Gardener*, Francis Lincoln, 2008

George F. Chadwick, *The Works of Joseph Paxton*, Architectural Press, 1961

Jennifer Davies, *The Victorian Kitchen Garden*, BBC, 1987

Brent Elliott, *Victorian Gardens*, Batsford, 1986

Caroline Holmes, *Victorian Gardens*, Schiffer Books, 2004

Caroline Ikin, *The Victorian Garden*, Shire Library, 2012

Caroline Ikin, *The Kitchen Garden*, Amberley Publishing, 2017

Justin Jennings, *Victorian Gardens*, Historic England, 2005

Judith Tankard and Martin Wood, *Gertrude Jekyll at Munstead Wood*, Pimpernel Press Ltd, 2015

20th Century

Jane Brown, *The Modern Garden*, Princeton, 2000

Susannah Charlton & Elain Harwood (Eds), *100 20th-Century Gardens and Landscapes*, Batsford, 2021

Fergus Garrett, *Great Dixter Then & Now*, Pimpernel Press, 2021

Wendy Hitchmough, *Arts and Crafts Gardens*, V & A Publications, 2005

Catherine Horwood, *Beth Chatto: A Life in Plants*, Pimpernel Press, 2019

Gertrude Jekyll and Lawrence Weaver, *Gardens for Small Country Houses*, Newnes/Country Life (4th Ed.) 1920

Gertrude Jekyll, *Colour Schemes in the Flower Garden*, Newnes/Country Life (3rd Ed.), 1914

David Ottewill, *The Edwardian Garden*, Yale, 1989

Graham S. Pearson, *Hidcote*, National Trust Books, 2013

Tim Richardson, *The New English Garden*, Frances Lincoln, 2013

Jesse Sheeler, *Little Sparta: A guide to the garden of Ian Hamilton Finlay*, 2015

Barbara Simms, *John Brookes, Garden and Landscape Designer*, Conran, 2007

Acknowledgements

The Gardens Trust would like to thank all those who have helped create this book by contributing text or photographs, and sharing their expertise. We would also like to thank Nicola Newman, Katie Hewett, Sally Bond and the team at Batsford, our editor Susannah Charlton and editorial panel Sally Jeffery, David Marsh and Jill Sinclair.

Harry Beamish is Chair of the Northumbria Gardens Trust and a historic environment consultant.

Andrea Bennett is Senior Gardener for the National Trust at Scotney Castle Gardens

Jane Bradney is a freelance garden historian and lecturer specializing in the 19th century and is the archivist of the Enville Estate.

Katie Campbell is a writer, garden historian, lecturer and tour guide who has taught at Birkbeck, Bristol and Buckingham universities.

Claire de Carle is Chair and Trustee of the Buckinghamshire Gardens Trust.

India Cole is a PhD researcher based between Queen Mary University of London and Oxford Botanic Garden.

Stephen Daniels is Emeritus Professor of Cultural Geography at the University of Nottingham and has published extensively on the history of landscapes and gardens, with a particular focus on their art and design in Georgian Britain.

Penny David worked in publishing for many years specializing in garden books. The formation of the Welsh Historic Gardens Trust led to a new career writing about old gardens.

Sarah Dickinson, former Trustee of the Gardens Trust, Chair of Surrey Gardens Trust and a doctoral researcher at University of Buckingham, considering the history, impact and significance of the planting plan.

Christopher Dingwall is a landscape historian, heritage consultant and lecturer. He is Honorary Research Advisor with Scotland's Garden and Landscape Heritage.

Annabel Downs is a landscape architect, garden designer and researcher and is current Chair of the Friends of the Landscape Archive at Reading.

Brent Elliott is a garden historian, lecturer and formerly librarian of the Royal Horticultural Society.

Jill Francis is an early modern historian, specializing in gardens and gardening in the late 16th and early 17th centuries. She has taught history at the universities of Birmingham and Worcester, and is currently helping to deliver the Garden Trust's online lecture programme.

Linden Groves has worked in the landscape conservation sector for 20 years and is Head of Strategy and Operations for the Gardens Trust. She is currently writing a history of playgrounds.

Paula Henderson is an architectural and garden historian, lecturer and writer. She has worked as a consultant and expert witness for historic gardens including Bramshill.

Clare Hickman is a Reader in Environmental and Medical History at Newcastle University and a Trustee of the Gardens Trust.

Virginia Hinze is a landscape architect specializing in restoring and managing historic designed landscapes; she is currently a Trustee of Sussex Gardens Trust

Marcelle Hoff is a garden historian whose MA was on the architect F. Inigo Thomas as a proponent of the concept of the garden in relation to the house.

Margie Hoffnung is Conservation Officer for the Gardens Trust and Chair of the Gloucestershire Gardens and Landscapes Trust. She previously worked at Westonbirt Arboretum and Highgrove, and with Rosemary Verey.

Caroline Holmes is a garden historian, author of 12 books, a consultant landscape designer and has lectured on every continent except Antarctica. www.horti-history.com

Catherine Horwood is a social historian and author with a particular interest in women in horticulture. Her biography *Beth Chatto: A Life with Plants* won the European Garden book of the year in 2019.

Peter Hughes KC is Chairman of the Gardens Trust. After retiring from the judiciary, he gained an MA in Garden and Landscape History, and looks after an Arts and Crafts house and garden in the Lake District.

David Jacques, OBE, is a garden historian and author and a cultural landscape specialist.

Fiona Jamieson is a former garden historian who has written on the gardens of Drummond Castle and the Palace of Holyroodhouse. She was also gardens and landscapes contributor to the Oxford Companion to Scottish History (2001).

Sally Jeffery was architectural and garden historian at the City of London, helped to set up the Birkbeck MA in Garden History, and until recently taught garden history at the Institute of Garden History. She is now an independent scholar.

David Lambert is Director of the Parks Agency and a lifelong believer in public parks and what they mean.

Jennie Macve is a landscape historian and Trustee of the WHGT. She worked as researcher and administrator for the Hafod Trust, and is the author of its guidebook, *The Hafod Landscape*.

Marion Mako is a garden historian, planting designer and tour leader, and a Trustee of Painswick Rococo Garden Trust.

David Marsh is Course Director for an MA in Garden History and an honorary Senior Research Fellow at the University of Buckingham. He gives regular talks, and writes a weekly blog for the Gardens Trust.

Michael McNaught is Derby Arboretum Park Manager.

Mark Newman is the archaeological consultant for the North Region (East) of the National Trust.

Nick Owen sits on the committee of Northumbria Gardens Trust.

John Phibbs runs a landscape consultancy specializing in the conservation and management of historic parks and gardens, and has particular expertise on the work of Capability Brown and Repton.

Sophie Piebenga is a gardener and garden historian. She is the Gardens' Archivist at Waddesdon Manor and leads garden tours both in Britain and abroad.

Paul Rabbitts works as Parks and Open Spaces Manager at Norwich City Council. He is a Trustee of the Gardens Trust and an author, parks historian and public speaker.

Tim Richardson is a garden writer, historian and critic, and author of numerous books on landscape design and garden history.

Barbara Simms is the Editor of *Garden History*, journal of the Gardens Trust, and was director of MA courses in garden and landscape history at the Institute of Historical Research and University of London.

Jill Sinclair is a garden historian, author and lecturer. She teaches the history of landscape gardens for Oxford University, is a Trustee of the Gardens Trust and a former Chair of Sheffield Botanic Gardens.

Ann Steele is Head of Gardens and Designed Landscapes for the National Trust for Scotland.

Lucy Stewart is historical researcher for Cowden Japanese Garden.

Michael Symes is an author and lecturer specializing in 18th-century gardens. He founded the Masters in Garden History at Birkbeck and is a Vice-President of the Gardens Trust.

Alan Taylor is Chair of the Staffordshire Gardens and Parks Trust.

John Watkins is Head of Gardens and Landscapes for the English Heritage Trust.

Twigs Way is a garden historian, researcher, consultant and speaker in garden history and designed landscapes.

Elisabeth Whittle is Chair of the Cambridgeshire Gardens Trust, Vice Chair of Hobson's Conduit Trust and a Trustee of the National Botanic Garden of Wales. She also serves on the conservation committee of the Gardens Trust. She was formerly Inspector of Historic Parks and Gardens for Cadw.

Tom Williamson is a landscape historian and landscape archaeologist whose research interests include the designed landscapes of the 18th and 19th centuries. He is Emeritus Professor at the University of East Anglia.

Jan Woudstra is Reader in landscape history and theory at the University of Sheffield.

Picture Credits

The Gardens Trust is the UK national charity dedicated to protecting and conserving historic parks, gardens and designed landscapes.

We bring together people from all backgrounds united by a love of historic parks and gardens to campaign for their protection, undertake research and conservation, encourage public appreciation and support community involvement.

Together with the network of County and Country Garden Trusts (CGTs), we provide expert advice through the planning system to help owners and local planning authorities manage change in historic parks and gardens. Our casework team and CGT volunteers deal with thousands of planning cases every year. Our research helps to ensure that significant gardens are added to Historic England's Register of Parks and Gardens of Special Historic Interest.

We could not do all this without the support of our members, donors and tireless volunteers. To join the Gardens Trust and get involved visit thegardenstrust.org

First published in the United Kingdom
in 2024 by
Batsford
43 Great Ormond Street
London
WC1N 3HZ

An imprint of B. T. Batsford Holdings Limited

ISBN 978 1 84994 903 3

A CIP catalogue record for this book is available from the British Library.

10 9 8 7 6 5 4 3 2 1

Reproduction by Rival Colour Ltd, UK
Printed by Toppan Leefung Printing International Ltd, China

This book can be ordered direct from the publisher at www.batsfordbooks.com, or try your local bookshop

The publishers have made every effort to trace the copyright holders and obtain permission to reproduce the images included in this book and apologise for any unintentional omissions. Please do get in touch with any enquiries or information relating to images or rights holders.